Let Their People Come

P
LET THEIR
eople
Come

*Breaking the Gridlock on
International Labor Mobility*

Lant Pritchett

CENTER FOR GLOBAL DEVELOPMENT
Washington, D.C.

Let Their People Come: Breaking the Gridlock on International Labor Mobility
may be ordered from:
BROOKINGS INSTITUTION PRESS
c/o HFS, P.O. Box 50370, Baltimore, MD 21211-4370
Tel.: 800/537-5487, 410/516-6956; Fax: 410/516-6998; Internet: www.brookings.edu

Library of Congress Cataloging-in-Publication data

Pritchett, Lant.
  Let their people come : breaking the gridlock on international labor mobility / Lant
Pritchett.
      p.   cm.
  Includes bibliographical references and index.
  ISBN-13: 978-1-933286-10-5 (pbk. : alk. paper)
  ISBN-10: 1-933286-10-5 (pbk. : alk. paper)
  1. Labor mobility. 2. Emigration and immigration—Economic aspects. 3.
Unskilled labor. I. Title.
  HD5717.P75 2006
  331.12′791—dc22   2006025112

9 8 7 6 5 4 3 2 1
The paper used in this publication meets minimum requirements of the
American National Standard for Information Sciences—Permanence
of Paper fo Printed Library Materials: ANSI Z39.48-1992.

Cover photograph: © Ann Johansson/Corbis

Cover by Sese-Paul Design

Typeset in Minion

Composition by Circle Graphics
Columbia, Maryland

Printed by Victor Graphics
Baltimore, Maryland

Center
for Global
Development

The Center for Global Development is an independent, nonprofit policy research organization dedicated to reducing global poverty and inequality and to making globalization work for the poor. Through a combination of research and strategic outreach, the Center actively engages policymakers and the public to influence the policies of the United States, other rich countries, and such institutions as the World Bank, the IMF, and the World Trade Organization to improve the economic and social development prospects in poor countries. The Center's Board of Directors bears overall responsibility for the Center and includes distinguished leaders of nongovernmental organizations, former officials, business executives, and some of the world's leading scholars of development. The Center receives advice on its research and policy programs from the Board and from an Advisory Committee that comprises respected development specialists and advocates.

The Center's president works with the Board, the Advisory Committee, and the Center's senior staff in setting the research and program priorities and approves all formal publications. The Center is supported by an initial significant financial contribution from Edward W. Scott Jr. and by funding from philanthropic foundations and other organizations.

Contents

FIGURES

Preface

The Center for Global Development (CGD) is a think tank and policy group focused on the ways that the policies and actions of the rich world spur or impede the pace of development in the poor world. Aid, debt relief, more open markets for developing country exports: these are universally seen as "development" issues, and they generate, if not consensus, then at least a fully shared framework within which debate takes place.

The cross-border movement of people is a different kettle of fish. In an increasingly integrated and liberalized economy, with more open capital and goods and services markets, the highly restricted and heavily regulated markets for global labor are an oddity. Moreover, with huge differentials incomes for equally productive people simply because of where they live; with international and internal migration offering individuals one of the few nearly sure-fire ways to escape poverty, with migrant remittances from rich to poor countries exceeding foreign aid; and with rich countries designing immigration policies to selectively attract the poor world's most talented and motivated people—with all this it is obvious that international migration and global labor mobility truly are "development" issues.

Even so, it was and is controversial for the Center for Global Development to foster work on international migration for three reasons. First, many in the development community did not, and do not, regard the movement of people as "development." For them, development takes place *within* countries or nation-states. The movement of people across borders—no matter their success in a new setting—is a symptom of failed development, not a contribution to sustained transformation of the third world.

Second, the politics of labor and migration policy in rich countries are so hugely contentious that it is reasonable to wonder whether smart new analysis of the issue from a development perspective could lead to better policies. Anti-immigration sentiment is rising in the United States and Europe. "Globalists" and rich world development advocates, who might otherwise support greater labor mobility for unskilled workers, hesitate given the potential negative effects on wages and income inequality in the receiving countries. And there is understandable ambivalence about the possible risk to poor countries of the so-called brain drain.

Third, the movement of unskilled or semi-skilled labor across borders from poor countries to rich countries disproportionately benefits three groups: those from the poor countries who move to higher wages; the richer part of the rich country population who benefit from lower wages for labor intensive services and whose wages are not threatened; and potentially labor intensive industries located in rich countries. This makes for an odd political coalition. Development advocates may have joined with people of faith to support debt relief, but a "development friendly" coalition of Oxfam and meatpacking plants in the Midwest is harder to envision.

The topic is too big to be ignored, however. From CGD's beginnings I resolved to exploit our advantages of analytic strength and political independence to put international migration and labor mobility more firmly on the global development agenda—even recognizing the limits of our potential influence on practical policy change. Our work on migration and labor mobility includes:

—The Commitment to Development Index, which ranks rich countries in terms of their policies and practices that affect development, "rewards" those countries with more open immigration policies for unskilled labor and for students.

—*Give Us Your Best and Brightest,* by senior fellow Devesh Kapur and his coauthor John McHale. Published last year, the book documents the growing competition of OECD countries for global talent, discusses how implications for poor countries differ depending on their circumstances, and proposes policies for the United States and other rich countries that respect the rights of talented people to move while also creating incentives for them to continue to contribute to their own country's development.

—An emerging body of work by CGD fellow Michael Clemens on the impact of emigration on developing countries' own prospects. His initial finding that emigration of African health professionals has no measurable effect on sending countries' health indicators is already reshaping the thinking of analysts and development practitioners. His work is also influencing U.S. legislative proposals on the issue.

To this solid body of work, I am delighted that we are now adding *Let Their People Come: Breaking the Gridlock on Global Labor Mobility*, an uncommon and exciting book by non-resident fellow Lant Pritchett. *Let Their People Come* examines the potentials and perils of greater cross-border mobility of unskilled labor—within poor world regions and between rich and poor countries. It is both a scholarly book and a fascinating read—with lessons for anyone interested in development and the global labor market, and for everyone interested in international migration more generally.

Pritchett portrays the cross-border mobility of unskilled workers and their families as occurring in the midst of a clash of "irresistible forces" and "immovable ideas." The irresistible forces include demographics (especially aging populations in the rich world and the need for young, tax-paying workers to keep the economy running and support retiree pensions) and the widening income gap between rich and poor countries. The immovable ideas are the anti-immigration sentiments of a large segment of rich country voters, who have legitimate concerns about the impact of low-skill migrant workers on public services, possible security risks, implications of the existing low-income workers, and potential cultural impacts.

But Pritchett also documents the tremendous gains to be had from greater labor mobility—gains that far outweigh the risks. All calculations suggest that even a very modest expansion in labor mobility can lead to economic gains for citizens of poor countries that far exceed all foreign aid, all the potential gains to the poor countries from the most optimistic Doha round scenario, and total debt relief. He makes proposals not for a new "global regime"—a politically unattainable goal in the foreseeable future—but for bilateral "deals" between rich and poor countries that set up ingenious arrangements for labor mobility, which would benefit not only those who cross borders to work but those they leave behind in sending countries, and those they join in the receiving countries.

Perhaps no other domain of the international system reveals that the world is not flat more profoundly than international migration and global labor mobility. The world is flat for goods, downhill for capital, but a steep uphill climb for workers—especially unskilled workers with the misfortune of not having been born with the right nationality. No other circumstance of birth—not race, gender, ethnicity, or parental socioeconomic status—so completely determines life chances as the nation of birth, essentially because of border restrictions on the mobility of labor. I feel certain that *Let Their People Come* will generate a new round of healthy debate on what should be seen as a critical and enduring development topic of this new century.

Nancy Birdsall
President
Center for Global Development
Washington, D.C.

Acknowledgments

This work was originally produced while I was on leave from the World Bank at Harvard University and as a fellow at the Center for Global Development. Hence, although I am currently an employee of the World Bank, no World Bank resources and no time of mine as a World Bank employee went into this book. Thus, the usual disclaimer about not reflecting the views of the World Bank or its member countries applies with even more than usual force. I would like to thank Nancy Birdsall for her support; Jeffrey Williamson for useful correctives; and William Cline, William Easterly, Michael Kremer, David Lindauer, David McKenzie, Mark Rosenzwieg, L. Alan Winters, and Michael Woolcock for helpful comments on a draft of the book. My daughter, Hannah Pritchett, provided research assistance throughout, but particularly on chapter 2. Finally, thanks to Dewi for walking and to Diane for walking and listening.

Let Their People Come

Introduction: Breaking the Gridlock on Labor Mobility

Some years ago, Nancy Birdsall was putting together a new think tank to support work in global development. The group was to be focused on promoting development, not by giving advice to poor-country governments—heaven knows, they get enough of that—but by examining the ways in which the rich countries of the world could do more (or at the least do less harm). Then as now, the standard mantra was "Fairer trade, better aid, and debt relief."

At the time, I said that another issue had to join this troika—labor mobility. The principal way rich countries disadvantage the poor world is not through unfair trade, or through intrusive and ineffective aid, or by forcing repayments of debts. The primary policy pursued by every rich country is to prevent unskilled labor from moving into their countries. And because unskilled labor is the primary asset of the poor world, it is hard to even imagine a policy more directly inimical to a poverty reduction agenda or to "pro-poor growth" than one limiting the demand for unskilled labor (and inducing labor-saving innovations). I asked this question: Why, when influential policymakers and advocates speak about "development," could we not hear a quartet, not just a trio; to fairer trade, better aid, and debt relief, add more access to rich countries for unskilled labor.

Little did I know just how right and how wrong I could be. I was absolutely right that immigration issues would come onto the

1

policy agenda. I have been absolutely wrong that (so far) that this could be a positive thing. As I finish this monograph, the United States is in the throes of a deep and contentious debate about immigration policy—and a recent Zogby Poll has "immigration" ranking right after terrorism and the war in Iraq as a concern among U.S. voters. The United Kingdom has recently announced policies that, except for EU workers, make access to it much more difficult for unskilled workers. In the wake of the spring 2006 riots in France, the interior minister was floating ideas about "toughening" up on immigration. The "development round" of World Trade Organization talks has almost no content concerned with increasing labor mobility. The only "pro-immigration" moves are those that expand the welcome mat for the very highly skilled—computer programmers, Ph.D. scientists, medical personnel. Labor mobility is in a policy deadlock—it has been growing, but in ways that are leading to more controversy and conflict.

The rich countries of the world should actively look for ways to increase the mobility of unskilled labor across their national boundaries. They should do this primarily because it is the right thing to do, because of the enormous potential benefits to people who are allowed to move. The rich countries can allow labor mobility that is both consistent with their own economic interests and "development friendly"—that is, labor mobility benefiting not only the nationals but nations. The economics of labor mobility are simple: Because gains from exchange depend on differences and, in today's economy, the same worker can make enormously higher wages in one location than in another, the gains from moving are obvious. The difficult part is political: How can development-friendly labor mobility policies that are politically acceptable to voters in rich countries be devised? The *ideas* of rich-country citizens—for instance, the idea that immigration will harm the poor in rich countries—are *the* obstacle to larger mutually beneficial flows of labor between rich and poor countries. Increased labor mobility will have winners and losers in rich countries—which is true of nearly every economic policy—and the key is to minimize the perceived losses to the poor citizens of rich countries.

Normatively, I am primarily concerned with raising the well-being of the world's least well off—not just the "poorest of the poor" but all people whose standard of living (which includes monetary and nonmonetary dimensions) is below that of those below the poverty thresholds of the world's rich countries, which is the large bulk of the world's population (Pritchett 2006). Most analysis and recommendations about the policies of the rich countries presume that policies should be informed exclusively by the interests of the current citizens of those countries (for example, Borjas 1999). But it is perfectly possible, indeed plausible, that the "best" policy determined by the interests of rich-country citizens makes the poor of the world worse off. I am interested in a different question: What are the policies toward labor mobility that would be most beneficial to the world's currently poor (who nearly all reside in poor countries) and yet are still politically acceptable in rich countries?[1] This is presuming at least some small degree of concern for the rest of the world in the making of rich-country policy—which clearly exists in humanitarian relief, in support of foreign aid (through both bilateral and multilateral agencies), in the movement for debt relief, in the granting of trade preferences, and in some aspects of international peacekeeping. Put another way, in the range of policies that rich countries are willing to implement at least putatively to benefit the world's poor, what is the scope for development-friendly policies toward labor mobility?[2]

Some simple numbers make the politics of the policy predicament clear. The industrial world currently transfers something on the order of $70 billion a year in overseas development assistance.[3] The magnitude of the beneficial impact of this aid in immigrant-receiving countries is hotly debated, but let us assume that the voluntary and mainly altruistic transfer of the $70 billion leads to roughly $70 billion in benefits for poor-country citizens. A recent World Bank study (2005a) has estimated the benefits of the rich countries allowing just a 3 percent rise in their labor force through relaxing restrictions. The gains from even this modest increase to poor-country citizens are $300 billion—roughly four and a half times that magnitude of foreign aid. What does

---

1. Note that in discussing "labor mobility," I am consciously distinguishing labor mobility, which may or may not even grant access to the recipient country's labor market, from "immigration" policy, which addresses claims on political rights or citizenship. Though these are often thought to be bundled together so that the ability to provide labor services and full political citizenship are thought of as a single decision, I will argue that policies toward "labor mobility" and "migration" can, and should, be separated *because* it will be good for the poor. Unfortunately, it becomes pedantic to always use "labor mobility" or variants (for instance, what is the "labor mobility" equivalent of calling an arriving person a "migrant"?). So, unless otherwise noted, "migrant" and "migration" are used in the broadest possible sense to include all cross-border movement, whereas "immigration" policy refers to those that may involve eventual citizenship or permanent residency.

2. There are enormous issues surrounding migration within regions in the developing world that make many countries both senders and recipients of migrants, but I will not deal with "South–South" flows at all.

3. The World Bank's World Development Indicators 2005 put the total world flow of "net official development assistance or official aid" at $58 billion in 1998 and $77 billion in 2003. The Development Assistance Committee put "official development assistance" from members to part I countries at $69 billion. I say "on the order of" because combining grants and concessional loans into the net present value of transfer terms is complicated, and not really necessary for the purposes of this book.

it cost the rich countries to achieve these massive gains? Actually, according to these same estimates, the current rich-country residents *benefit* from this relaxation on distortions to labor markets—so the net cost is in reality a net *benefit* of $51 billion. It would seem that the choice between spending $70 billion on foreign aid for an uncertain magnitude of gains versus a policy change with a net benefit to rich-country residents of $51 billion for gains to the world's poor of $300 billion would, naively, be an easy one.[4] The crude "cost-effectiveness" of gains to the poor per aggregate cost to the rich country is *infinitely* larger. But rather than increasing commitments to expanding labor mobility as a complement to assistance, one estimate is that the total spent by just five industrial countries on *preventing* these labor flows is $17 billion (Martin 2004)—a substantial fraction of what they spend to help others.

It is not puzzling that there is little policy advocacy for increased labor mobility as a means of benefiting the rich countries. Those who would oppose relaxing restrictions can easily point out that the purely economic gains to the rich countries are small—even $51 billion is indeed a tiny fraction of the industrial countries' aggregate gross domestic product of $32 trillion—and the social and distributional consequences are mixed. But what *is* puzzling is the traditionally deafening silence about rich-country policies from those who are concerned about the world's poor compared with the literatures on aid and trade. The potential gains to poor-country citizens from even small increases in labor flows are much bigger than anything else on the international agenda—either aid or trade. Yet institutional, academic, and popular advocacy from the "development community" has been almost exclusively about improving financial flows (either more or better) or about reducing the trade barriers of rich countries.

Of course, pretending this is a puzzle is itself naive; it is really not so puzzling: National and international politics keep some things on the agenda and other things off it. But there is nothing unique about the politics of labor mobility, and nearly all the objections that "explain" why labor mobility is not on the agenda could be applied to liberalizing trade in goods—but in other cases do not preclude policy. When the topic of labor movement arises, some object that some people in rich countries are hurt by allowing in more labor. That same is true of free trade. The recent campaign to emphasize the harm done to African cotton growers by cotton subsidies to American farmers acknowledges that American farmers would be harmed by a reduction in their subsidies—but this is a political obstacle to be overcome,

---

4. Other estimates, which make different assumptions about rich-country labor markets, find benefits of $156 billion for a gain of $7 billion to permanent residents of rich countries.

not a reason to not advocate the reduction in subsidies. Many point out that increased labor mobility is unpopular with voters—but again, often so is free trade, yet that is seen as an obstacle to be overcome in the interests of a desirable policy rather than as a reason to not discuss liberalizing trade. Many point out that there are "social" consequences of labor mobility—but just ask anyone from Detroit or Pittsburgh if there are social consequences of free trade. But again, the consistent response in the case of free trade is for the advocates of free trade to find ways to address the political objections—through "safeguards," through the mitigation of the social consequences, through international mechanisms that harness national politic interests, through tireless documentation of the potential gains—in the pursuit of what the advocates believe are policies that lead to overall gains. The economics is easy—the gains are there; the politics of policy is hard.

From opening thesis sentence to the conclusion, this brief monograph is primarily policy advocacy.[5] The structure is simple. First, I argue that there are five *irresistible forces* creating growing pressures for the greater mobility of persons across national boundaries in search of economic opportunities in the twenty-first century. Second, these irresistible forces are being held in check by eight *immovable ideas* of rich-country citizens, who use coercion to block cross-national labor mobility. Third, I propose six *accommodations*, elements of rich-country policy toward unskilled labor mobility that might break the policy deadlock and reconcile the irresistible forces and immovable ideas while still producing policies that are development friendly.

Five Irresistible Forces

The five large and growing forces that make the pressure for mobility across national boundaries greater than ever before in human history are:

—*Gaps in unskilled wages.* Wage gaps of between 2 to 1 and 4 to 1 between immigrant-sending and -receiving countries were sufficient to cause massive migration flows, even with the conditions of transportation and com-

5. This is not primarily a review of the academic literature about the effects of migration. Hatton and Williamson (2006) provide an excellent summary of what is known about the effects of migration in the "first globalization" period before the closing of borders in the 1920s and 1930s. The World Bank's regular *Global Economic Prospects* report for 2006 was devoted to migration, with new estimates of gains, an excellent review of the literature, and a focus on remittances. The International Organization for Migration (2005) published *World Migration 2005: Costs and Benefits of International Migration*, which also has excellent reviews of the literature on effects and on remittances. For a much broader view of the economic and social effects of migration, see Massey and others, *Worlds in Motion: Understanding International Migration at the End of the Millennium* (1999).

munication in the nineteenth century. The real wage gaps between potential sending and receiving countries are much larger today than a hundred years ago—often as high as 10 to 1. These wage gaps create pressure for migration because they are *not* primarily explained by differences in the characteristics of *people*. Wage rates are predominantly characteristics of *places*: People who move tend to have earnings much nearer the average wage of the country they move to than they are from, even in the short run.

—*Differing demographic futures.* The now-rich countries of Europe and North America, as well as Japan, have demographic futures that are very different from other countries near them. This is starkest comparing Europe and its periphery. The labor-force-age population of Italy is forecasted to shrink from 39 million to 26 million from 2000 to 2050, while the labor-force-age population of Egypt will expand from 40 million to 83 million—a change from one Egyptian worker for every Italian worker to *three* Egyptian workers for every Italian worker. Because it is a fundamental principle for economists that differences create trade, these increasing differences will create ever greater pressures for labor flows—both pressures in Europe to accept greater labor flows and pressures for outward flows in sending countries.

—*The globalization of everything but labor.* Though migration has increased, particularly migration to rich industrial countries, the increase in the mobility of labor has been small compared with the greatly increased flows of goods, capital, and ideas and communication across national boundaries. Globalization has now reached the stage where the economic gains from the further liberalization in goods or capital markets are impressively tiny compared with the gains from the increased mobility of labor.

—*The rise of employment in "low-skill, hard-core nontradables."* The results of increased productivity, rising incomes, aging populations, and the globalization of manufacturing imply that much of the incremental growth in the labor force will be in what I call "hard-core nontradables"—that is, services (nontradables) that cannot be outsourced and that do not require a high skill level. According to the projections of growth in demand for specific occupations made by the U.S. Department of Labor, more than half the labor demand growth in the top twenty-five occupations (5 million jobs) will occur in this category. Though modern economies will need more computer engineers and postsecondary teachers, they will also need more home health aides, janitors, cashiers, and fast food workers.

—*Lagging growth in "ghost" countries.* Chapter 2 presents an important fifth force for greater labor flows, and it is a chapter all its own because, though chapter 1 mainly synthesizes existing information, chapter 2 presents new research. The fifth force for greater labor flows is that there are large negative and positive changes in the economic prospects of specific geographic regions, and these create pressures for migration. Large and persistent declines in labor demand in a region, perhaps because of technical changes in agriculture or changes in resources, create two possibilities, which I call "ghosts" or "zombies." If labor is geographically mobile and hence labor supply is elastic, then large declines in labor demand will lead to large outward migration—the process that created "ghost towns" in the United States. However, if labor demand falls in a region and labor is trapped in that region, by national boundaries for instance, the labor supply is inelastic and all the accommodation has to come out of falling wages. A region that cannot become a ghost (losing population) becomes a zombie economy—the economy might be dead, but people are forced to live there.

Chapter 2 presents evidence from comparisons of countries of the world, from regions of the United States, and from historical experiences that there are in fact large, region-specific changes over time in labor demand and that, when migration is possible, this creates massive migration flows. The chapter then also illustrates how large the pressures for outward migration due to the actual population exceeding the "desired" population might be. One concrete example illustrates the point. There is a contiguous collection of counties in the Great Plains region of the United States that had more than a million people in 1930 and whose *absolute* population in 1990 had both fallen by 27 percent and was also only 36 percent of what it would have been without outward migration. But with this outward migration, per capita income has grown at roughly the rate of the rest of the United States. In contrast, Zambia's per capita income peaked in 1964, and in 2000 was only 60 percent of its peak. But during that same period, its population has grown from 3.5 million to 10 million. It is not really difficult to believe that the negative shocks to Zambia's economy have been as large as those of the U.S. Great Plains region and that if labor were mobile, the population dynamics would have been similar. Even if Zambia were to adopt policies that resume growth, the pressures for outward migration would still be enormous—the population of Zambia would be only *a fourth* its current level if its outward migration matched that of the Great Plains.

Eight Immovable Ideas

These five powerful forces for the greater movement of people have created some increases in migration, but only a small fraction of the potential, and the mobility of people across national boundaries is held in check by ideas. Let us not be squeamish: The real barrier to the movement of people across national boundaries is *coercion*—people with guns stop them. The fact that the coercion is civilized, legal, and even polite should not prevent us from naming it coercion. This exercise of nation-state coercion to prevent labor flows is under the complete and total control of the democratic processes in rich countries. Hence the real barriers to increased labor mobility are the *ideas* of these rich countries' citizens. There is no question that in nearly all rich countries migration is *very* unpopular—in a number of opinion surveys, fewer than one in ten people in many countries belonging to the Organization for Economic Cooperation and Development favor increased migration.

Chapter 3 reviews the eight ideas that underpin resistance to increased labor flows. These ideas appear immovable because they are difficult and painful to address head-on, and nearly everyone would prefer to not explicitly confront them because they often go to very fundamental notions of justice and equity. I argue that many of these ideas are *myths*, in that they are symbolic narratives that rationalize actions often taken for very different reasons. The eight ideas are:

—*Nationality is a morally legitimate basis for discrimination.* Nearly every modern polity is now built around the notions of fairness and equity. Now, after centuries of struggle, it is widely regarded as morally illegitimate to limit people's life chances because they were born a woman, are of a minority race or ethnicity, were raised in a certain religion, or have a physical disability. And yet, as chapter 3 documents, the single largest factor affecting a person's life chances is the country in which he or she is born—this dwarfs gender or race or parents' socioeconomic status as a determinant of well-being. The notion that the differences in life chances resulting from being born in Mali or Nepal are morally legitimate is central to limiting migration.

—*There is a moral perfectionism based on proximity.* The second idea that underpins resistance to labor mobility is that proximity or physical presence in the same political jurisdiction is all that matters for moral obligations. As long as a specific Haitian is suffering while physically in Haiti, the moral obligation of the United States is nothing, or next to nothing. If that same Haitian manages to arrive on the soil of the United States, the moral obligation to that specific person increases almost infinitely. At the same time, it is perceived as moral to deploy violence to prevent that Haitian from setting foot on American soil by, for instance, interdicting his or her boat in international waters. All the countries with the highest ratio of foreign-born population legally (and in every other way) treat their guest workers as "second-class citizens." The uncomfortable fact is that this lack of a moral concern that depends on physical location—particularly the fact that the moral concern is always low—makes the workers better off. The oil-rich Gulf states have a ratio of foreign-born to domestic population larger than most European countries by an order of magnitude;

and while in these countries, the guest workers do not acquire any citizenship claims at all. So the fact that the typical Gulf state citizen feels no moral obligation to a Bangladeshi if they are in Bangladesh and no moral obligation to the Bangladeshis even if they are physically in the Gulf state makes the Bangladeshis much better off because they are allowed access to the Gulf state's labor market in quantities that would be unthinkable if they had to be treated politically as equals. Though free immigration that includes the acquisition of citizenship rights and the modern welfare state might be incompatible, greater labor mobility and the modern welfare state are not.

—*"Development" is exclusively about nation-states, not nationals.* The third idea is that "development" must be only about the fate of those who remain within the borders of their nation-state. Not surprisingly, given that international organizations are precisely that, the interests of nation-states dominate global forums. Because the primary benefit of labor movement accrues to the person who moves rather than to the sending or receiving nation-state, if "development" is about the living standards of nationals, then labor mobility is obviously a desirable policy for development. However, if one construes "development" to be only about the interests of nation-states, then "migration" is often perceived as something to be minimized or eliminated. The governments of nation-states have, for a variety of reasons, much more interest in what happens to the incomes of the people (and firms) that reside within the geographic space they control than in the well-being of all "nationals." This leaves the international system and all its agencies (whose members are typically nation-states) almost exclusively concerned with what happens within *national* boundaries. It is easy to find out from a stream of data sets emanating from international organizations about the well-being of individuals who now live in Jamaica, El Salvador, Armenia, or Ukraine. But what is the average income or well-being of *Jamaicans, Salvadorans, Armenians,* or *Ukrainians* (defined as either those born in those countries or those that self-identify with them)? No one knows.

—*Labor movements are not "necessary" (or desirable) to raise living standards.* The fourth idea that underpins restrictions on labor mobility is the notion that it is not really necessary for development. In particular, two ideas take labor mobility off of the table. One is that the movement of people is unnecessary because trade in goods can lead to the equalization of wages—factor price equalization—without it. The second is that movements of capital—either as aid or private capital flows—can substitute for the movement of people in equalizing wages across countries.

In addition to the ideas about what is normatively "right," there are also the politically much more important ideas about how migration affects the self-interest of rich-country voters. Four important notions underpin the resistance to increased labor mobility based on self-interest:

—*Increased migration of unskilled labor will lower wages (or take jobs away from natives) and worsen the distribution of income in the receiving countries.* One influential idea that limits migration is that increased flows of unskilled labor will be bad for the unskilled labor already in the country. Unlike many of the other ideas, this idea—grounded in simple demand and supply—is almost certainly true. But though this is an enormous concern and needs to be addressed directly, it does not preclude well-designed, development-friendly labor mobility policies. The economists' usual response to distributional arguments against efficient policies is "instruments to targets," and for economists to resist migration on this ground while advocating free trade is intellectually inconsistent. Second, this is only true if the impact is not mitigated—any serious proposal for increased migration needs to address the distributional effects head-on.

—*Movers are a fiscal cost because they use more services than they pay in taxes.* A common fear is that newly arrived immigrants will use more public services than they will pay for in taxes and hence constitute a fiscal burden. Whether this is true or not is a complex question, but it does inspire anti-migrant policies, such as those aimed at limiting access to services for migrants or their children.

—*Allowing movement across borders creates risks of crime and terrorism.* Obviously, in the wake of not just the tragic events of September 11, 2001, in the United States but also the train bombings in Madrid of March 11, 2004, and the July 7, 2005, subway and bus bombings in London, the terrorism implications of cross-border movements of people are a first-order issue. No proposal that does not take into account these security concerns (as well as concerns about street crime) is going to be politically viable in the near future.

—*"They" are not like "us"—culture clash.* Perhaps the main political driving force against increased migration is the cultural argument that allowing the physical presence of others who do not share the same value systems would undermine the "cultural cohesion" of the existing society.

Six Accommodations for Politically Acceptable, Development-Friendly Migration

Because the main forces blocking increased labor mobility are ideas, the most important agenda is to develop ideas—proposals for the national and international agendas that create development-friendly policies toward migration and create sustained pressures for the adoption of these proposals. Chapter 4 proposes six "accommodations"—aspects of proposals for greater labor mobility that are both *politically acceptable* to voters in rich countries and also *development friendly.* I argue that these six accommodations are necessary because the two major existing trends in migration policy are either not development friendly or are not likely to be politically acceptable.

As documented in Kapur and McHale's *Give Us Your Best and Brightest* (2005), one trend in migration policy in countries belonging to the Organization for Economic Cooperation and Development is a move toward restricting migration or, if continued or increased levels of migration are contemplated, adopting policies that lead to "higher-quality" immigrants by placing more emphasis on skills. Though this emphasis on the contributions of potential migrants can lead to greater political acceptability (in part because it avoids downward pressure on unskilled wages), it is almost certainly less "development friendly" than allowing greater numbers of less-skilled migrants. There are obvious benefits to "brain circulation" that might offset the traditional fears of "brain drain," but it is almost certainly the case that if rich countries choose exclusively those migrants of higher productivity and grant them permanent status, this pattern of the "three Rs" (recruitment, remittance, and return) is less favorable for the migrant-sending countries than policies emphasizing remittances and return.

The other potential trend is toward bringing labor mobility under the World Trade Organization (WTO). I argue that the existing WTO is unlikely to be the focal point for substantially increased flows of unskilled labor. The principles that make the WTO (and its predecessor, the General Agreement on Tariffs and Trade) a good forum for negotiating reductions in trade barriers—most-favored-nation policies, price-based interventions in trade, and reciprocity—lead to politically unacceptable outcomes when applied to labor mobility.

A politically acceptable and development-friendly scheme for labor mobility should include six features:

—*Bilateral, not general multilateral, agreements.* These agreements will be between pairs or small sets of countries. There is little or no prospect for binding multilateral commitments or open arrangements. For security as well as historical and "culture clash" reasons, most host countries will engage in agreements that include only selected nationalities (and ration among those).

—*Temporary status for labor mobility.* The tide has turned toward using skills as a criterion for immigration policy (those admitted permanently)—with many countries adopting policies intended to decrease the number of unskilled or low-skilled migrants (by reducing "family reunification" and asylum as modes of immigration). Hence the best hope for the increased admission of unskilled labor is labor mobility through temporary agreements—in spite of the risks this entails for political backlash.

—*Rationing, using specific quotas (by job and perhaps region)*. Although economists would nearly always prefer prices over quantities as a means of regulation, politically only carefully controlled numerical allocations that use deliberative mechanisms to address fears of "taking away jobs" are likely to succeed.

—*Enhance the development impact on the sending country*. Because migration in the first instance benefits nationals while many conceive of development as about nation-states, development-motivated labor mobility policies should include ways of enhancing the perceived development impact. One objection must be addressed: In bringing labor mobility onto the development agenda, the maximum additional labor that would be accommodated is so small that the benefits would be concentrated on only a few citizens of poor countries, like a labor lottery.

—*Involvement of the sending country in enforcement*. One major concern of any scheme for temporary migration is that liberal democracies are incapable of adequately enforcing such agreements unilaterally. Sending-country cooperation can greatly assist in making temporary schemes feasible.

—*Protection of the fundamental human rights of migrants*. This is not an "accommodation" but also a fundamentally desirable feature of any program for labor mobility. No one is more vulnerable than a person far from home who does not understand the language and the legal system, and who is often outside any social support network (because migrants often work alone) and is seen as ripe for exploitation by employers and traffickers. To be politically acceptable in rich countries, programs need to emphasize that people coming to perform unskilled labor are not making "tragic choices" from economic desperation (as they at times are when migration is made illegal) but are making positive choices in which their dignity and rights are maintained.

In discussing how the wealthy countries of the world can assist in the development of the rest of the world, the policy agenda has often been dominated by aid and trade. In fact, there is a sense that some hope more generous aid and freer trade could make migration—which is politically a much more highly charged issue—completely unnecessary. Migration policies in some instances are even perceived to be working against development goals. But after half a century of aid-centered development policies and programs combined with a gradual but now nearly complete "globalization of everything but labor," the global system should now be ready to bring labor mobility fully onto the agenda. For this to produce positive outcomes, there must be sustained attention to the design and implementation of schemes that can accommodate the mounting irresistible forces against the immovable opposition of rich-country citizens' ideas.

1

Four Irresistible Forces for Increased Labor Mobility

F our irresistible forces today cause observed increases in labor mobility—and each promises to become even more powerful in the future. These forces are wage gaps, demographics, "everything but labor" globalization, and the services future of labor demand in industrial countries. A fifth force—rapid and massive shifts in the desired populations of various countries—has the next chapter to itself. Four preliminary observations are useful:

—The current differences in unskilled wages, or wages adjusted for skill, are more than twice as large as those that set the world in motion in the late nineteenth century. This wide divergence of the incomes of the poorest and richest countries has created enormous wage gaps for both skilled and unskilled labor, and the migration pressure in these gaps is almost certain to increase.

—A fundamental principle of economics is that differences create opportunities for exchange. The rich countries, particularly the European nations and Japan, have embarked on a historically unique demographic trajectory of increased longevity and fertility rates below the level of population replacement. During the next half century, this will produce ratios of the retiree-age population to the labor force–age population unlike those ever experienced. At the same time,

these countries' geographic neighbors are projected to have large and growing populations of youth. This difference in potential labor will produce
another irresistible force for increased labor mobility.

—Unlike the first era of globalization, the post–World War II era has been
an experiment in "everything but labor" globalization. But once everything
else is global—communications, financial flows, ideas, goods—the losses
from cross-border mobility to the mover become smaller and the gains from
increased labor movements become more and more obvious—and less and
less possible to resist.

—The gains in employment in rich countries are increasingly in service
sectors that are "hard-core" nontradables—for example, personal services
like haircuts and home health care and truck driving. Although "outsourcing" as a new phenomenon has received the lion's share of attention in recent
years, I argue that it will remain quantitatively much smaller than the services
that require physical presence.

Irresistible Force One: Large and Increasing
Wage Gaps across Countries

Although people make complex choices about where to move that depend on
many social, cultural, and familial factors, if all else is equal, an increase in the
gap between what people earn where they are now and what they could earn
by moving increases the *pressure* for mobility. With sufficiently low incomes,
people may not be able to afford to move so that increased gaps—particularly
if they result from falling incomes of the poor—may not result in increased
mobility. This may also mean that decreases in the wage gap as a result of
increases of the incomes of the poorest countries may actually result in greater
realized labor mobility.

However, before addressing that complication, let us review evidence of
three types, which lead from the familiar (differences in income across countries) to the relevant (gaps in wages for the same worker across countries,
adjusted for education and skills). First, the massive historical increase in the
income gap between rich and poor countries means that the gaps in income
across countries are now much larger than gaps *within* countries. Second,
massive income gaps could potentially reflect differences in capital or rents to
resources rather than wages, but the current gaps in unskilled wages (either
in nominal terms or adjusted for purchasing power) between many potential
immigrant-sending and -receiving countries are substantially larger today
than in the "age of mass migration." Third, income or wage differences across
regions create mobility to the extent that people can change their earnings

by moving. It is possible that cross-national differences in wages are entirely explained by cross-national differences in worker characteristics, such as education, and hence are irrelevant for worker mobility. But, in fact, nearly all of the earnings gap between workers in poor countries and rich countries appears to be due to their *location*, not their personal characteristics.

Divergence and Income Gaps across Countries

The typical person in a rich industrial country lives better in *material* terms than any king or duke or the wealthiest financier in 1820 or even 1870.[1] The suburban chariot—the ubiquitous minivan—provides safer, faster, and more comfortable travel than the grandest carriage ever built. Cellular telephone owners can pull from their pocket a device that can communicate more quickly and reliably with any corner of the globe than anything available to the most powerful world leader in 1900. Nearly every house in the developed world has flush toilets connected to an amazing system of waste treatment and disposal that eliminates the stench and disease that afflicted even the wealthiest in the nineteenth century. In the age of digital recordings, people have access to a wider variety of better-performed music anywhere they travel than the richest of courts could ever provide. Health conditions have improved enormously so that nearly every child in the industrial world is born with a better chance to reach adulthood than the richest could achieve.[2]

This enormous transformation has been brought about by the gradual, but cumulatively explosive, improvement of material well-being in those countries at the top of the world distribution of income. According to conventional measures, output in most of the currently industrial countries has grown steadily at about 2 percent a year at least since 1870—so that today average incomes are ten to fifteen times higher (Maddison 1995). However, not all countries have participated in this growth. In many countries, incomes are still very low—not only lower than those of the industrial countries today but also lower than the industrial countries' level in 1870. The combination of steady growth at the top with many countries lagging at the bottom has

---

1. I emphasize "material" because there are many ways in which the human condition is unchanged or has changed for the worse. I am not convinced people are nobler, braver, more moral, or imbued with a deeper artistic and sense of the humane today than historically (and I am convinced I personally do not possess these compared with persons in the past in the relative abundance that I possess better lawn mowers). Moreover, while science has progressed, the loss of metaphysical certainty and the concomitant sense of personal security and social identity have both pluses (more tolerance of deviation) and minuses.

2. Not only do I not have to worry about infectious diseases and epidemics, but genetic defects that are easily operable today would have killed the children of even the most favored.

Figure 1-1. *Inequality in Incomes over Time, Showing Trend from Differences of People within Countries and Differences across Countries, 1800–2000*

Percent of total inequality due to differences

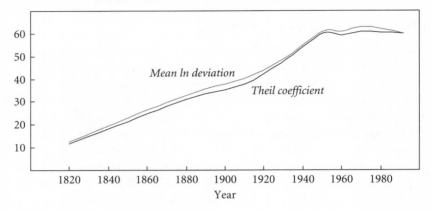

Source: Bourguignon and Morrison 2002.

caused a historical "divergence big time" (Pritchett 1997). The ratio of incomes between the top and bottom countries has increased from 10 to 1 in 1870 to something like 50 to 1 today.

Bourguignon and Morrison (2002) have undertaken the heroic exercise of examining the evolution of the *personal* distribution of income over a very long time scale. Their estimate is that in 1820 only about 10 percent of the differences in incomes among all individuals in the world were due to differences in average incomes across countries.[3] In 1820 it did not really matter that much whether one was a peasant in England, India, or Ethiopia—life was hard, and the gap *within* each country between the rich and poor was substantial. But most of the inequality in the world today is because of differences in incomes across countries, because the fraction of the world's income inequality that is accounted for by differences *across* countries has grown from 10 to 60 percent and remained at this level (figure 1-1).[4]

---

3. Actually, due to the lack of availability, they divide the world up into groups of countries. The "across"-country gap would be even larger for actual countries.

4. According to their calculations, this ratio has held steady in recent periods, which, because their estimates are of the personal distribution of income and hence are population weighted, is consistent with the rapid growth in China and India (Sala-i-Martin 2002).

This gap in incomes across countries has, in most regions of the world, continued to grow rather than shrink. While the two largest countries, India and China, have grown faster than the average for countries belonging to the Organization for Economic Cooperation and Development (OECD) and hence converged on the leaders, many countries have seen the gap between their income and that of the leaders grow larger in recent decades. This growing gap is a feature of many bilateral relationships between potential immigrant-recipient and -host countries. Figure 1-2 shows the evolution of the ratio of per capita gross domestic product (GDP; this time, in exchange rates adjusted for purchasing power parity, or PPP, so the ratios are much higher but unaffected by trends) between various pairs of countries linked by proximity or historical or cultural ties. Mexican output per person peaked at 50 percent of the U.S. level but fell back to about 40 percent, where it had been

Figure 1-2. *Evolution of the Ratio of Per Capita Gross Domestic Product (GDP) between Pairs of Countries Linked by Proximity or Historical or Cultural Ties, 1955–2000ᵃ*

Ratio of GDP per capita, PPP

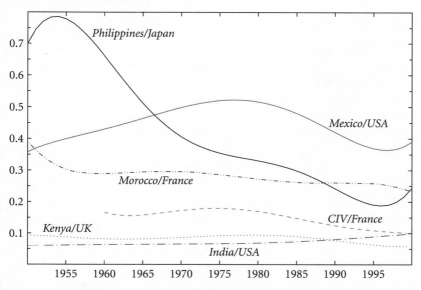

Source: Author's calculations with Penn World Tables 6.0 data on per capita gross domestic product. Ratio is smoothed with a cubic.

a. GDP is in exchange rates adjusted for purchasing power parity, or PPP.

in the 1950s. The Philippines' output per person has fallen from almost 80 percent of Japan's output in the post–World War II period to about 30 percent today. Morocco's output per person has fallen gradually, but steadily, to only 25 percent that of France. Note that while the largest country, India, is booming, its level of output per person has reached only 10 percent that of the United States—and a fourth that of Mexico.

Gaps in Wages

Gaps in income per capita across countries are only suggestive of migration pressures, because the relevant question for a worker is the difference in wages that he or she would earn in the two countries. We will start looking into this with cross-national differences and then move to direct comparisons. Using a recent data set on wages and hours in the industrial sector across countries (Rama and Arcetona 2002), one can create comparisons of wages per hour in industry across countries. Unadjusted for PPP, wages differ enormously between the OECD countries and the low-wage countries near the OECD countries. In these data from the late 1990s, wages in Japan are $13.32 an hour, compared with 13 *cents* an hour in Vietnam—a ratio of 100 to 1. Wages in the United States are $13.64 an hour, versus 76 cents an hour in Guatemala, a gap of 18 to 1. Even comparing an OECD country like Spain with a middle-income country like Morocco, industrial wages differ by a factor of 7 (figure 1-2).

Comparing wages at official exchange rates is not the right comparison for considerations of labor movement, for two reasons. First, prices tend to be lower in poorer countries, and hence official exchange rates overstate differences in the value of consumption from an hour's wage for a worker. Second, moreover, comparing the "industrial sector" across two countries' workers is problematic because the countries' sectors differ in composition and skills. Because the PPP calculations often seem opaque, a simple example helps illustrate the realities of the comparison of wages based on their purchasing power in command over consumer goods. How many minutes of a construction laborer's work are required to purchase a kilogram of wheat flour? While an American construction laborer works less than 4 minutes to earn enough to buy a kilogram of flour, it takes a Mexican worker more than 1 hour and an Indian construction worker just under 2 hours.

What do the fully corrected PPP comparisons suggest are the wage gaps across potential migration partners? And how would we know if these gaps are "big enough" to overcome the many frictions to labor movement? It is well known that in the period of open migration in the nineteenth and early twentieth centuries there was massive labor mobility. Though it is difficult to make

Figure 1-3. *Ratios of Wages of Immigrant-Sending and -Destination Partners during the Era of Mass Migration Compared with the Ratios of Wages of Potential Sending and Destination Partners Today*[a]

Ratio of wages in PPP

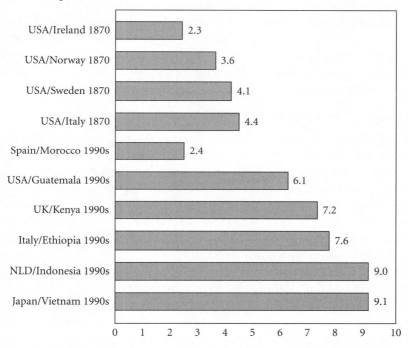

Sources: O'Rourke and Williamson 1999 (wages in 1870); Rama and Arcetona 2002 (wages in 1990s).

a. Ratios of wages adjusted for purchasing power parity, or PPP, of the United States and its migration partners in 1870 and pairs of countries in the 1990s.

real wage comparisons,[5] it appears that the wage differentials that set in motion the mass migrations in the late nineteenth century are substantially smaller than the current gaps in real wages between potential migration partners. Figure 1-3 compares the ratios of PPP-adjusted wages of immigrant-sending

5. We are comparing the O'Rourke and Williamson (1999) real wages of unskilled laborers—often taken from data on the building trades and adjusted for prices—with the wages in all the industrial sectors in the 1990s adjusted for purchasing power parity (PPP) using the price levels from the Penn World Tables 6 (http://pwt.econ.upenn.edu/). There are many reasons why these two—historical data on wages of unskilled laborers and current data on industrial wages adjusted for PPP—are not perfectly comparable.

(Ireland, Italy, Sweden, Netherlands) and the United States partners during the era of mass migration with the ratios of wages adjusted for PPP of potential sending and destination partners today. The wage ratios between Japan and Vietnam (9.1 to 1), the United Kingdom and Kenya (7.2 to 1), or the United States and Guatemala (6.1 to 1) are substantially larger today than the historical ratios between the mass senders and the United States (Ireland, 2.3 to 1; Sweden, 4.1 to 1). In many ways, figure 1-3 is central: We know that the wage gaps in the late nineteenth and early twentieth centuries were sufficient to set the world in motion in an era of open borders. Yet the real wage gaps today across countries dwarf those of the era of mass migration.

What Do Migrants Earn When They Move?

Wage differences create pressures for labor mobility to the extent that they reflect differences in earnings potential for the same individual. The existing literature suggests that nearly all the differences in wages between individuals in rich and poor countries are explained by the *location* of the worker, not their personal characteristics. When workers move, their earnings look much more like the earnings of workers in the country they move to than where they moved from.

Thousands of empirical studies of the determinants of individual earnings have established that individual characteristics like education, labor market experience, physical strength, and even birth weight correlate with earnings. But on reflection, two points are obvious. First, given the magnitudes of these estimated effects *within* national labor markets, these forces can explain only a tiny fraction of observed wage gaps *across* countries. That is, given the simple Mincer earnings specification that schooling increases earnings proportionately and that the wage increment to a year of education is something like 10 percent,[6] then the ratio of the wage of a person with twelve years of schooling to someone with only six years (a primary education) is 1.8—compared with the national wage ratios in industry (which almost certainly substantially understate average national wage gaps overall) of 6 or 9 to 1. So whereas some of the wage gaps are explained by differences in observed individual characteristics, the differences in observed characteristics and the gaps these cause in national labor markets cannot come close to explaining the differences across nations.

Second, when wages are compared by educational level, then wages of immigrants look quite similar to those of natives with a similar education— and completely different from those with the same education in their coun-

---

6. This is near the average of the existing empirical studies (Pritchett 2004b).

try of origin. Table 1-1 presents just one illustrative example, comparing earnings of Salvadorans in El Salvador and in the United States. The ratio of wages of Salvadoran male workers with a secondary degree in the United States is *exactly* the same as the average for the U.S. population, whereas it is 8.5 times higher (unadjusted for PPP) than for workers with the same degree in El Salvador. This is just confirming the obvious, which is that the U.S. and Salvadoran labor markets are integrated within borders, so that equivalent workers make the same amount, while they are sharply separated by national borders, so that *equivalent* workers on different sides of the border can make completely different amounts.

More telling still, recent data on the earnings of migrants before and after migrating show that when they move, their wages are almost identical to those of workers in the country they move *to* and almost nothing like those in the country they move *from*. Jasso, Rosenzweig, and Smith (2003), using data on worker earnings before and after immigration to the United States, show an increase of $17,000 to $37,989 (in PPP) *for the same worker*—or, in other words, wages nearly double just by moving across the border.[7]

This is not to argue that new workers make immediately 100 percent of what equivalently educated and trained native workers make. There is a large economic literature on how quickly the wage gap between immigrant and native worker closes (if at all). The older conventional wisdom was that wage gaps closed almost entirely quite quickly, but this is being challenged by newer studies that find more persistent gaps, particularly with some ethnic groups. But by using data only from the host country (for example, the United States), one can easily miss the point about labor mobility pressures. That is, suppose that wages of workers with less than a high school education converged to only 80 percent of those of native workers with the same level of schooling. Though these may be interesting for a number of reasons for economic and social conditions in the United States, it still may be true according to simple

---

7. Of course, this still does not account for the fact that migrants are self-selected and hence the income gains might be overstated as more ambitious or able people move, so even comparing the wage before and after may overstate the gains of moving the "typical" worker. A study using a lottery for Tongans moving into New Zealand (McKenzie, Gibson, and Stillman 2006) found that (1) comparing wages in the two countries overstated the income gains, and (2) in fact the "before and after" overstated the "true" income gains. But the "true" pure income gains estimated using the "natural experiment" of a lottery was a 263 percent gain for the Tongans who moved. Of course, whether this "experimental" estimate of the gains of moving a typical Tongan or the observed "before and after" is relevant depends on whether one is interested in local average treatment effects (relevant if the current system expands at the margin so the incremental migrant is self-selected) or some average treatment effect (relevant only if one were going to allow a lottery to determine movement or a nonmarginal expansion).

Table 1-1. *Earnings of Salvadorans with Equivalent Levels of Education in the United States and in El Salvador*

| Level of education | Average annual earnings of male workers aged 25 to 40 in El Salvador (dollars)[a] | Average annual earnings of male workers (dollars) | | Ratios of earnings of those workers | |
		Salvadorans in U.S	U.S. average	Salvadorans in El Salvador / Salvadorans in U.S.	Salvadorans in U.S./ U.S.average
None	2,289	16,686	10,243	7.3	1.6
Completed primary school	1,263	18,529	7,106	14.7	2.6
Completed secondary / high school degree	2,669	22,611	22,087	8.5	1.0
University degree	9,246	27,893	38,363	3.0	0.7

Sources: Calculations from 2000 U.S. Census; 2002 Encuesta de Hogares de Propositos Multiples (National Household Survey) for wages in El Salvador.

a. 2002 dollars not adjusted for purchasing power.

arithmetic that movers have enormously higher wages in the United States than in their home country. Just using round numbers, if wages for unskilled labor are $10 an hour in the United States and $2 an hour (adjusted for PPP) in another country, then even if newcomers only ever make 80 percent of the U.S. level, the wage is $8 an hour, which is four times higher than wages in the country of origin, something that can never be revealed using only U.S. wage data comparisons.

Gaps as a Force for Migration

The gaps between what workers make in one country and another is clearly an irresistible force impelling greater labor mobility across national boundaries. The migrations from Europe to the areas of recent settlement—the United States, Canada, and Australia, as well as Argentina and Brazil—in the era of open migration (among these countries) are well documented. In the forty years from 1870 to 1910, labor flows were truly massive for the receiving countries and for some (but not all) of the sending countries. The increase in the size of the labor force due to migration was 21 percent for the United States, 40 percent for Australia and Canada, and 80 percent for Argentina. Conversely, the cumulative impact of migration was to *decrease* the size of the labor force in Norway and Sweden by respectively 22 and 18 percent, in Italy by 29 percent, and in Ireland by 41 percent (table 1-2).

Workers who are "unskilled" by rich-country standards, that is, who have little education, can earn enormously more by working in a rich country than in nearly any poor country. The wage gaps in the world today are at historically high levels. The massive migrations of the nineteenth century were propelled by wage differentials between sending and recipient countries of between 2 to 1 (United States / Ireland) and 4 to 1 (United States / Italy, United States / Sweden). Today there are PPP-adjusted differences among workers in

Table 1-2. *Migration in the Era 1870–1910*[a]

Percent

Country	Adjusted net migration rate labor force	Adjusted cumulative impact on the labor force
Argentina	13.95	75
Canada	8.22	39
Australia	7.85	37
United States	4.78	21
Belgium	1.98	8
Brazil	0.88	4
France	−0.12	0
Germany	−0.86	−3
Netherlands	−0.71	−3
Portugal	−1.26	−5
Spain	−1.38	−5
United Kingdom	−2.67	−10
Denmark	−3.2	−12
Sweden	−4.99	−18
Norway	−6.24	−22
Italy	−8.54	−29
Ireland	−13.35	−41

Source: Hatton and Williamson 1998.
a. Migrants as a fraction of population based on per 1,000 migrants per year in the labor force.

the industrial sector between potential sending and recipient countries (based on geographic proximity or historical ties) of 6 to 1 (United States / Guatemala), 7 to 1 (United Kingdom / Kenya), or even 9 to 1 (Japan/Vietnam).[8] If a wage gap of 4 to 1 between the United States and Italy in 1870 was sufficient to create a migration that reduced population by 30 percent over a forty-year period[9]—even when transport costs were higher, travel was more dangerous, and communication with loved ones left behind was much more expensive and less reliable—then it is at least plausible that the existing wage differences indicate potential forces for substantially larger labor movements than those currently observed.

There are two major caveats to this use of the gaps in wages as an index of the irresistible force for migration, both of which are important but neither of which undermines the basic message of large and increasing labor movements. First, there is a distinction between the *pressure* for labor movements and the *propensity* to move. Though the *pressure* for migration might be a monotonic function of the gap in a worker's wages between two locations, the *propensity* to migrate depends on the worker's ability to actually undertake a long-distance move. If there are large fixed costs to migration and borrowing to finance these costs is costly or impossible to arrange, then the poorer and destitute cannot afford to move (Faini 2001). Much, though not all, of the empirical literature examining actual movements within and across countries, and using the historical data (Hatton and Williamson 2006), is consistent with the view that the propensity to migrate at first *rises* with rising income. As incomes increase from very low levels, more people are able to respond to the pressure for movement and actually move.

---

8. As large as these differences are, there are two ways in which they likely *understate* the relevant comparison for many migrants, for three reasons. First, these are comparisons between industrial workers in both locales and hence probably understate the average wage gaps economywide as workers in agriculture or informal services in developing countries make much less than industrial workers, a gap that is much smaller in a developed economy. Second, even the adjustment for PPP is not enough; and even if PPP wages were equal, the worker in the poor country has a "better" lifestyle in material terms. Comparisons of non-money measures of well-being (health, education) or of food share, however, do not suggest that the PPP comparisons are wildly wrong, as the nonmoney metric indicators suggest lower standards of living for the relatively well off in poor countries than for the poor in rich countries (Pritchett 2006). Third, adjusting wages for PPP assumes that the relevant prices are in the country in which the wage is earned—but if a worker is remitting, say, a third or half of his or her income for consumption of household or family members at home, then part of the wage is buying consumption at the lower prices of the country the worker comes from and hence *household* utility is higher.

9. This also assumes similar ratios for other countries receiving Italian migration.

How does the introduction of the *absolute level* of wages of the potential migrant as an additional factor in the pressure of a wage differential between locations in the overall propensity to migrate change the basic story? This obviously complicates scenarios for the future, for one now has to think of the effects of wage growth in potential sending countries both as it affects the threshold and as it affects the wage gap. For the poorer countries, where wage gaps are large, there are three scenarios. First, wages fall in absolute terms, which leads to an increase in pressure but reduces the capability to move. Empirically, this could go either way. Second, wages rise, but less than those in rich countries. In this case, the two effects reinforce each other as the slow wage growth gives more and more people the capability to move while the wage gap increases the pressure. Third, wages are rising more than in rich countries. In this scenario, it depends on the strengths of the two offsetting effects, but in poor countries the effect of rapid wage growth in giving more and more people the capability to move is likely stronger than the reduction in gap effect (as the gaps are very large) and hence could increase the propensity even as the pressure declines. The fact that the wage gap between Mexico and the United States (one of the world's largest bilateral migration flows) is substantially *smaller* than most other wage gaps (for example, much smaller than between India and the United States) suggests that income-induced pressures are bound to rise even with rising wages in most poorer countries—even those gaining on the leaders (table 1-3).

The fact that falling wages, say in Africa, could mean less pressure for migration as fewer people have the capacity to move is not an attractive long-run proposition, and there are two choices. The first is that this is a temporary phenomenon and wages will begin to rise again in Africa, which means that people will be crossing the threshold level of being able to afford migration in a future where wage gaps are even larger, which implies that the falling wages will only postpone the time for large migration pressures. Or second, Africa remains too poor to create substantial migration pressures forever—and the relative gaps get wider and wider—not a prospect to be desired by anyone.

The second caveat is that by emphasizing the role of wage differentials as one of the forces driving movements of persons, we do not want to suggest that all movement of people is economically motivated, and do not want to suggest a crude caricature of economics—that even those economically motivated decisions are determined exclusively by a desire to maximize current income. For instance, some sociologists, such as Douglas Massey, who have studied migration argue that many economic migrants have something like a "target accumulation" motivation—that is, their decision to move to a high-earnings labor market is not with the goal of remaining there but rather as a

Table 1-3. *Scenarios for Wage Growth in Poorer Countries and Implications for Pressure (Wage Gaps), Thresholds, and Propensity to Migrate*

Assumed wage growth in poorer country ($\dot{w}_{rich} \approx 2ppa$)	Wage gap (pressure)	Wage gap currently large (> 4) or small (< 4)	Effect on propensity from crossing threshold	Net effect on propensity from pressure and threshold
$\dot{w}_{poor} \leq 0$	Grows	Large	Reduces, big	+/– Propensity could decrease even as wage gap rises (for example, Africa)
		Small	Reduces, small	+/– Propensity likely rises as wage gap effect dominates (for example, in parts of eastern Europe)
$0 \leq \dot{w}_{poor} \leq \dot{w}_{rich}$	Grows	Large	Increases, big	+/+ Propensity increases from both forces (for example, Latin America)
		Small	Increases, small	+/+ Propensity increases from both forces (for example, in parts of eastern Europe)
$\dot{w}_{poor} \geq \dot{w}_{rich}$	Falls	Large	Increases, big	–/+ Propensity could rise even as wage gap falls as more people can afford to move (for example, in India)
		Small	Increases, small	–/+ Propensity likely falls as reduction on gap effect dominates (for example, in parts of eastern Europe)

Source: Author's calculations.

way of accumulating a stock of savings, perhaps for marriage, to buy a house or a piece of property, or to start a business in their home country. Given the variety of migrants from different countries and to different countries, coming from a variety of ages and family situations (some young and single, some married with children), it is plausible that "target accumulation" with return is a motivation for at least some migrants. If this is the case, then an increase in wage differentials might have complex effects on the flow and stock of migrants. The flow of migrants would almost certainly increase—as the number for whom either higher earnings or target accumulation is attractive rises—but the stock of foreign workers in the recipient country would not rise by as much as the flow, because the target accumulation would happen faster. It is even conceivable that the total stock would decrease, but I know of no particular evidence that this has ever been the case.

Irresistible Force Two: Differing Demographic Futures

A second irresistible force for increased labor flows is the radically different demographic futures implied by at least the current differences in birthrates. Nearly all European countries—some more rapidly and dramatically (for example, Italy and Germany) than others (for example, France and the United Kingdom)—are embarked on a truly remarkable demographic experience. The current UN population projections imply that the labor force of many European countries and Japan will not just cease to grow but decline in absolute terms by substantial amounts. Though national populations have stagnated or declined before due to excess deaths (for example, the Black Death) or out-migration (for example, Ireland), absolute population declines because people have decided to have fewer children than the replacement level are historically unique. The neighbors of Europe and Japan still have fertility rates well above replacement levels.

These differing demographic futures imply two things. First, the relative populations of regions will shift massively. Second, the changes in the labor-force-age population, and particularly the young population, will change even more dramatically, creating a "youth dearth" in some countries and a youth bulge in others.

Evolutions of Population

The United Nations' latest projections of populations suggest that the labor-force-age (fifteen to sixty-four years) population of many European countries and Japan will be substantially smaller in the future. The populations of Germany, Japan, and Italy have already begun to shrink and, for Italy and Japan, are projected to be only 60 percent of their 2000 size by 2050. France and the United Kingdom will remain roughly the same size during the next fifty years. Among large industrial countries, only the United States is expected to continue to experience sizable population growth (these projections already assume some level of migration).

Europe's neighbors, conversely, have not yet had similarly large shifts in fertility, and these differences imply enormously different demographic futures. In a recent paper, Demeny (2003) has illustrated the consequences of the current projections, particularly for Europe and its periphery. He compares the population of Europe (defined to include twenty-five countries in the broad definition of Europe) and that of its "Muslim tier" with the countries from North Africa to the Middle East to West Asia that surround Europe. In 1950 Europe had roughly twice the population of these neighbors (360 million compared with 180 million). Sometime in the late 1980s, these neighbors passed Europe's population, and by 2025 the tables will be completely turned and the Muslim tier will have twice the population of Europe. If one continues the projection to 2050, Europe's Muslim tier will have three times the population of Europe—1.2 billion to 400 million (figure 1-4).

Figure 1-4. *The Relative Populations of the European Union (25 Members) and Its "Muslim Tier," 1950–2050*

Population (millions)

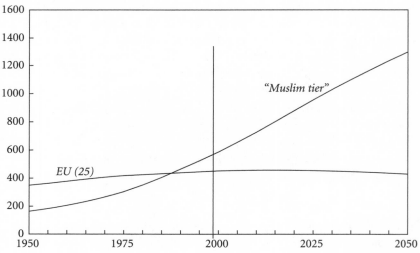

Source: United Nations Department of Economic and Social Affairs 2002 (Paul Demeny seminar slides)

Youth, and the Lack Thereof

What makes these demographic changes even more dramatic is what they imply for the age structure of the population. The population pyramids (the population in each age group) of European countries will "invert," so that instead of the traditional broad-based pyramid with more young than old, in the future the population pyramid will be standing on its tip. Figure 1-5 shows the population pyramid for two of the more dramatic examples: According to the projections in Italy, by 2050 there will be nearly *twice as*

Figure 1-5. *Projected Demographic "Pyramids" for Japan and Italy, 2050*

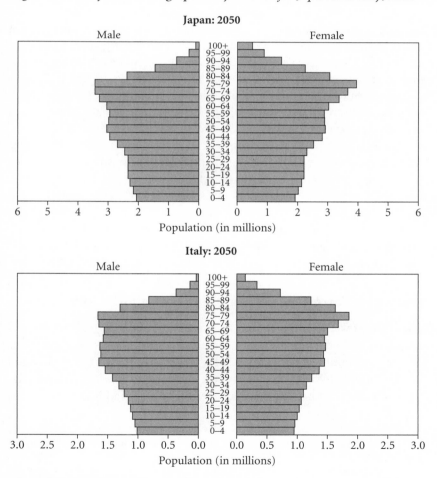

Source: U. S. Census Bureau, International Data Base.

many women age seventy-five to seventy-nine years as there are girls age zero to four—many more grandmothers than granddaughters. In Japan, there will be many more women over seventy than in the entire childbearing years.

This contraction in youth relative to the total population has several implications. The most obvious is for the financial viability of the current pension and social transfer schemes. The implications for the "support ratio" of labor-force age to the "retirement-age" population are staggering. Current projections show support ratios falling in Germany from 4 to 2, and in the more dramatic cases of Italy and Japan they fall to about 1.5—only 1.5 workers for every retiree. The systems of social transfers in Europe can be sustained only with very high tax rates even at *current* support ratios and program design parameters (which include a combination of tax rates, ages, benefits, and so on). But if support ratios fall to anything like projected levels, then it is not clear that there are politically feasible combinations of design parameters that can make the systems solvent—either tax rates need to be too high or retirement benefits drastically curtailed.

This is not to suggest that migration is *the* solution to the problems of an aging population. Suppose the projections for the rate of natural increase in the rich countries extend into the future: If the labor force increased sufficiently to keep support ratios constant at their current values, how large would the fraction of the labor force that was "foreign born" be in 2050? For Japan, well over half the population would be foreign born, and near half for Italy and Germany. It is very difficult to believe that these societies would allow anything like this level of labor mobility

A fundamental principle of economics is that differences create incentives for exchange. The enormous demographic differences between rich countries and their neighbors increasingly create incentives for labor flows.[10]

Irresistible Force Three: "Everything but Labor" Globalization

The third powerful force behind increased migration is that the world is becoming more connected in every other way—trade in goods, movements of capital, communications, travel. This creates two pressures for increased labor mobility. It lowers the relative cost of moving by making moving relatively less costly both in financial and psychic terms. In addition to lowering

---

10. One interesting fact, noted in Birdsall and Pritchett (2002), is that the implications for the United States are less dramatic than for Europe or Japan. Fertility has not fallen as rapidly or as far in the United States, and the demographic behavior of the "natural" immigration partners of the United States shows lower fertility rates than does that of the countries in proximity to Europe or Japan.

the costs to movers, on the policy level the question arises: If everything else is globalized, then why not labor?

The Costs of Being a Migrant Are Lower

The changes in the world resulting from globalization have also lowered the cost of being a migrant, in nearly every way. Most obviously, travel times are shorter, so there are fewer labor days forgone in traveling to and from work. Even in the late nineteenth century, when ships were the only form of travel and ocean passage took weeks, wage differentials and seasonal changes in labor created seasonal migrations, perhaps most famously in the *golodorinas* (swallows) who traveled back and forth from Italy to Argentina. Today, similar trips can be made in hours.

One of the costs of long-distance labor mobility is being out of touch with friends and family. Today, telephone calls make communicating with loved ones back home much easier. The international media, including the Internet, make staying in touch with events "back home" much easier. With freer movement of goods and lower transport costs, movers also no longer have to do without their favorite food, music, or clothing. Making remittances today is much easier (though the industry can still be high cost when competition is limited; see World Bank 2005a).

The literature on migration has documented the importance of "network" effects—that migrants are likely to move to a place where there already is a familial or ethnic connection. These network effects arise both from labor markets (because jobs are often found through personal connections) and also from the mitigation of the social and psychic costs of migration. It is clear that the slower but steady growth of labor movements and migration with the globalization of everything but labor creates an enormous momentum for greater migration. An initial enclave can create links that—through more complete connections of people, information, and finance—create the pressures for even greater migration. Though this was in evidence in historical migrations (Hatton and Williamson 2006), it likely operates even more effectively today.

Why Not Labor?

The international system has created a mechanism for negotiating reductions in trade barriers. Relative to its stated objectives, this has been enormously successful. One could argue that this international system is a victim of its own success and has created the conditions in which labor mobility must emerge on the global agenda. Winters and others (2002) have used a general equilibrium model to estimate gains from increased labor mobility. These calculations have two very important points, the magnitude and the distribution.

First, an expansion in labor mobility of the magnitude of 3 percent of the labor force in host (labor-importing) countries (an additional flow of around 16 million people) would lead to world welfare gains of $156 billion.[11] Although a smallish (0.6 percent) fraction of world GDP, this is larger by nearly a factor of *three* than annual official development assistance in the 1990s and substantially larger than the same model's estimate of the gains from *all* proposed remaining trade liberalization ($104 billion).[12] These estimates are, if anything, conservative.

The World Bank's *Global Economic Prospects* report for 2006 focuses on migration. It uses the Bank's standard general equilibrium model, LINKAGE, and estimates that for the same increase in the developed-country labor force (3 percent) the gain is more than twice as large, $356 billion, as the estimates by Winters and others (2002).[13] The exact calculations depend on assumptions about wage gaps between sources and hosts of movement and the modeling of labor markets, in particular how "subsititutable" domestic workers and movers are, but in the end some simple arithmetic dominates. If, as the Jasso, Rosenzweig, and Smith (2003) estimates suggest, each worker gains $17,000 a year from the move, then 16 million people times that amount represents an annual gain of $272 billion.

Moreover, these calculations are comparing a modest increase in labor mobility to all (further) trade liberalization. Hamilton and Whalley (1984) calculate that free migration could as much as *double* world income—which makes it very hard to stay motivated about the fractions of 1 percent that further trade liberalization can generate. These empirical results make intuitive sense. Goods markets are in fact quite deeply integrated, and though there are still gaps across countries in prices and evidence that the "border" effects inhibiting trade are still quite large, the price differences in goods across countries induced by restrictions on trade are very small relative to the observed wage gaps of as much as 10 to 1. Because, in the standard economic "triangle" calculations, the efficiency losses rise with the *square* of the distortion, further liberalization of trade (where distortions have been reduced) just cannot

---

11. The general equilibrium effects are small relative to the direct effects. Total gains are $156 billion, which is a gain of $170 billion for those who move offset by a loss of $14 billion for those who do not.

12. Of course, there are other estimates of trade liberalization that are larger, depending on what is assumed about the accomplished trade liberalization and what is included (for example, Cline 2005).

13. Few of these general equilibrium estimates allow for capital mobility, so they are general equilibrium in that they account for shifts in relative prices (including the price of skills) but not necessarily all dynamic changes.

compare to gains from even small relaxations of restrictions on labor. Though labor mobility remains off the agenda, it is increasingly difficult to make a compelling case for additional reductions to barriers to markets for *goods*. More simple arithmetic illustrates the similar calculation for development assistance: Moving someone from making $2 an hour (in PPP) to making $10 an hour at 40 hours a week, 50 weeks a year, raises that person's income by $20,000 a year. All official development assistance is roughly $60 billion a year. Allowing an additional 0.5 percent of the rich-country labor force to enter from poor countries would produce gains in the monetary value of all official development assistance.

Figure 1-6 shows the gain (in percentage of world GDP) from full labor mobility, the estimate of 100 percent of GDP, versus the gains from continued trade liberalization (fractions of 1 percent of world GDP)—of course, the current World Trade Organization agenda cannot even be seen on this scale. But while comparing full labor mobility with free trade is facetious—it is worth understanding why. Although the world welfare gains are substantial

Figure 1-6. *Why Is this Graph Facetious? The Estimated Gains from the Liberalization of Labor Mobility Relative to Continued Trade Liberalization*

Gains as percent of world GDP

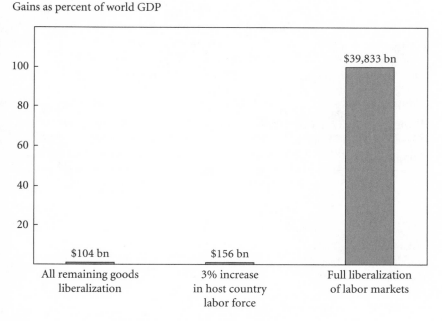

Sources: Hamilton and Whalley 1984; Winters and others 2003.

for an even modest relaxation of the constraints on labor mobility, a general equilibrium model that tracks the total impact of labor movement—the effect of wages and capital prices in the sending and receiving countries, and so on—reveals the fundamental difference between the globalization of goods and movements of labor. With movements of labor, nearly all the gains accrue to the *movers*—those who change their country of residence and hence will be concentrated (table 1-4). We return to this question about the distribution of gains below.

Irresistible Force Four: Continued Employment Growth in Productivity-Resistant, Low-Skill, Hard-Core Nontradable Services

Even in a high-technology, information-revolutionized, automated, capital-intensive, whiz-bang speed-of-business economy, a haircut is a haircut. A barber in the United States can give about as many haircuts an hour as he could a hundred years ago—and about as many an hour in the United States or Germany as in India or Eritrea. This is a "productivity-resistant" service. Though giving a haircut does require skill, it does not require years and years of formal schooling and can be acquired mainly through "on-the-job" experience. Haircuts cannot be "outsourced"—even with all the wonders of telecommunication and information technology, the scissors have to touch the hair. The key question is, how much of future employment growth in rich countries looks like "haircuts"—for which the only effective form of globalization is labor mobility—versus employment in tradable goods like manufacturing,

Table 1-4. *By One Calculation, More Gains from Labor Mobility Accrue to Those Who Move*
Billions of dollars

	Welfare gains		
Region or group	Home region	Temporary migrants	Permanent residents
Total world	156	171	−15
Developing countries	73	90	−17
Rich industrial countries	76	69	7
Eastern Europe and countries of former Soviet Union	8	13	−5

Source: Adapted from Winters and others 2002, table 2.

agriculture, or potentially tradable services? Perhaps counterintuitively, although the future belongs to greater and greater levels of technology, information revolution, and capital–labor substitution, the future of employment belongs to haircuts.

Table 1-5 illustrates this fact. It shows the U.S. Department of Labor's forecasts of the occupational categories with the largest *absolute* projected growth

Table 1-5. *Projections of the Top Twenty-Five Occupational Categories by Absolute Increase in Employment, 2000 and 2010*

Occupation	Employment in 2000 (thousands)	Employment in 2010 (thousands)	Projected Absolute increase (thousands)	Percent of the increase (of top twenty-five)
Combined food preparation and serving workers, including fast food	2,206	2,879	673	
Retail salespersons	4,109	4,619	510	
Cashier, except gaming	3,325	3,799	474	
Security guards	1,106	1,497	391	
Waiters and waitresses	1,983	2,347	364	
Truck drivers, heavy and tractor trailer	1,749	2,095	346	
Nursing aides, orderlies and attendants	1,373	1,697	324	
Janitors and cleaners	2,348	2,665	317	
Home health aides	615	907	292	
Laborers and freight, stock and material movers	2,084	2,373	289	

(*continued*)

Table 1-5. *Projections of the Top Twenty-Five Occupational Categories by Absolute Increase in Employment, 2000 and 2010 (continued)*

Occupation	Employment in 2000 (thousands)	Employment in 2010 (thousands)	Projected absolute increase (thousands)	Percent of the increase (of top twenty-five)
Landscaping and grounds keeping	894	1,154	260	
Personal and home care	414	672	258	
Receptionists and information clerks	1,078	1,334	256	
Truck drivers, light orderly services	1,117	1,331	214	
Packers and packagers, hand	1,091	1,300	209	
Total, hard-core nontradable services, low to medium skill	27,492	32,679	5,177	56.3
Registered nurses	2,194	2,755	561	
General and operation managers	2,398	2,761	363	
Postsecondary teachers	1,344	1,659	315	
Teacher assistants	1,262	1,562	300	
Total, hard-core nontradable services, skilled	7,198	8,737	1,539	16.7
Total, hard-core nontradables	34,690	41,416	6,716	73.1

(*continued*)

Table 1-5. *Projections of the Top Twenty-Five Occupational Categories by Absolute Increase in Employment, 2000 and 2010 (continued)*

Occupation	Employment in 2000 (thousands)	Employment in 2010 (thousands)	Projected absolute increase (thousands)	Percent of the increase (of top twenty-five)
Customer service representative	1,946	2,577	631	
Office clerks, general	2,705	3,135	430	
Total, potentially tradable services, low to medium skill	4,651	5,712	1,061	11.5
Computer support specialists	506	996	490	
Computer software engineers, applications	380	760	380	
Computer software engineers	317	601	284	
Computer systems analysts	431	689	258	
Total services, skilled	1,634	3,046	1,412	15.4
Total increase, top 25 occupations	40,975	50,174	9,189	100

Source: U.S. Department of Labor data.

in employment between 2000 and 2010. Though all forecasts have to be taken with a grain of salt, particularly of economic outcomes that are determined by markets in equilibrium, these projections do illustrate three features of the evolution of the advanced economies and hence of labor markets that are robust and have enormous implications for labor mobility.

First, though the growth in new and high-skill occupations will always get popular and media attention, the absolute level and absolute growth in lower-skill occupations—even though relative wage shifts in the United States show skill-biased growth. Table 1-5 lists four separate applications with computers (support specialists; software engineers, applications; software engineers; and systems analysts); all four of these employed 1.6 million people in 2000. These computer occupations are forecast to grow extraordinarily rapidly in percentage terms (many almost doubling in ten years), so that by 2010 employment will have nearly doubled to 3 million. But even so, in 2010, when there are 3 million people with advanced skills working in these high-tech computer-related occupations, there will be 3.4 million truck drivers, 5.2 million people serving food, and 8.4 million people working as cashiers or in retail sales.

Although perhaps initially counterintuitive, this is really not so puzzling. One of the key insights from economic models with differential sectoral rates of productivity growth is that the *low*-productivity-growth sectors come to dominate employment. This is known as the Baumol effect, after William Baumol (1967), who pointed out that because many labor-intensive services are "productivity growth resistant," their relative price goes up over time, and because fewer and fewer workers are required in the rapid-productivity-growth sectors, the share of services in total employment grows over time. The source of the Baumol effect is that some things are harder to automate or to replace capital for labor with than others.

But these projections of total employment could be totally wrong, or they could be irrelevant for pressures for labor mobility if services become "tradable." Media attention flows to the new and sensational, and hence news and reports about "outsourcing" have become all the rage—so much so that one might be tempted to think that the "world is flat" (Friedman 2005) or that location is irrelevant and hence outsourcing will reduce or eliminate pressures for labor mobility. But the new nearly always reflects the same principles as the old. What made something "nontradable" was the comparison of value in different places to the transport cost—so in history when transport costs were very high, only goods with a very high ratio of value to weight (like spices) were worth transporting, while as freight costs fell even bulk grains became tradable. Thus the dramatic fall in the cost of transmitting information means that a large range of formerly "nontradable" services that involve the exchange of information have become "tradable," and hence their production can move abroad in response to labor cost differences. Though this does lessen pressure for migration in those particular industries, one should not exaggerate the fraction of the economy to which this applies. A large range of services is still like the economists' prototypical "hard-core" nontradable: a haircut that still requires face-to-face (or, more precisely, hand-to-hair) contact.

I have classified the twenty-five occupations with the largest projected growth in employment in the United States into four categories based on my judgment of whether they are hard-core nontradables or potentially tradables ("outsourcable") and skilled or unskilled. Of the projected increase in 9 million jobs, almost three-quarters are, by my lights, in the nontradable category and 56 percent are in the nontradable and less skilled category. Though these are not the "glamorous" high-tech or skilled jobs, the fact of the matter is that the United States is going to need more home health care workers, more janitors, more security guards, and more fast food employees. The existence of massive numbers of low-skill, hard-core nontradable jobs in rich industrial countries is a fourth irresistible force for greater labor mobility.

Of course, the other way these projections of employment growth in hard-core nontradables could be wrong is if there is technical innovation that finds ways to replace these jobs altogether with machines or technology. There are already machines being developed that can, say, vacuum floors or deliver items within a workplace, and one can easily imagine in the not too distant future that taxi drivers could be replaced with global positioning systems and vehicles that are automatically piloted. I would like to point out the global perverseness of this innovation, driven as it is by the distortions in global labor markets. Let me illustrate with a story about my neighbor when I lived in Massachusetts, Paul Baratta, and his lawn mower.

One recent Saturday, I was reading papers about the historical evolution of global inequality when Paul called me to rave about his new lawn mower. He had nursed his old lawn mower along for twenty-five years (he is quite mechanical), but it (and he) had finally broken down and a new mower had been purchased. He was excited that for exactly the same *nominal* (not inflation-adjusted) price of about $400 that he paid twenty-five years ago he got twice the mower—almost twice the horsepower, self-propelled with a variable-speed transmission, a casing designed for air flow conducive to mulching, and so on. I shared his enthusiasm because, coincidentally, I had purchased the same lawn mower just a week before.

When I returned from lawn mower lauding with my friend Paul to reading about global inequality, I realized that this simple experience illustrated three important forces. First, for the entirely aesthetic care of our lawns, Paul and I deployed a greater capital stock than most rural households in poor countries deploy to earn their living. A rural household with access to a 5-horsepower mower is capital rich. The capital intensity in rich industrial counties is spectacular.

Second, Paul and I both mowed our lawns ourselves. Given the opportunity cost of our time and our willingness to pay, there are *billions* of people on the planet who would gladly mow our lawn for the price we would be willing to pay. Of course this raises in its starkest form the distributional issue to which we return in coming chapters, the issue that makes international mobility such a "third-rail" political issue: It benefits the globally richest (educated individuals like Paul and myself) and the globally poorest (migrants who would mow lawns) but has feared effects on the poorer in rich countries (existing migrants or natives who would mow lawns). But again (and I will return to it), the real threat to the working poor in rich countries is displacement by capital, not other labor.

However, the final insight from the technological advances of the lawn mower is that these advances required highly trained engineers working for years to make advances that made an owner-operated labor saving device better. This is nationally sound but globally perverse economics. Given the relative prices and endowments in rich countries, the incentives are to deploy very highly skilled labor to create innovations that *reduce* demand for low-skilled labor. In fact, there is substantial evidence that technical progress in rich countries has not been neutral between skilled and unskilled labor but rather has been skill enhancing. Moreover, this skill-biased technical change is induced by relative prices and accounts for a substantial fraction of the rise in wage inequality (and/or unemployment) in industrial countries (Acemoglu and others 2003).

The development literature points out that research in specific areas—such as agriculture or medicine—is biased away from the concerns of the poorer countries, because of differences in willingness to pay. So, for instance, there are innovative proposals to induce pharmaceutical companies to address major health issues facing poor nations because their market incentives are to focus on conditions that disproportionately affect the rich. But the distortion in the research and development induced by restrictions on labor mobility gets almost no attention and almost certainly has an impact that is *orders of magnitude* larger. The current configuration of the "everything but labor" global economy produces incentives for the invention of more and more *unskilled labor saving* devices in a world in which *the* key price for poverty alleviation is the wage of unskilled labor. Because of the artificially inflated price of labor in rich countries, the rich world is full of highly educated innovators dedicated, indirectly, to lowering the one price on which progress in poverty reduction depends.

Just think of the automated teller machine (ATM), which was invented and then diffused so as to reduce the labor content of handling routine banking transactions. There are almost certainly billions of people who would have been happy to take the jobs an ATM replaces, at wages that would make ATMs uneconomical. However, once the ATM had been invented, the fixed costs of its development borne, banking computing systems made consistent with it, and mass production begun so unit costs fell, then ATMs began to be present even where labor costs are extraordinarily low.

Once this perversity strikes you, it will strike you again and again if you live in a rich country (and particularly if one travels back and forth from poor to rich). In the cities of poor countries, it is not unusual for groceries to be delivered directly to your door. Even when I was a teenager (in the mid-1970s), many of my friends had jobs helping carry groceries to customers' cars. Now, many retail stores (grocery, hardware, general merchandise) are introducing automated checkout, whereby customers use sophisticated technology and invested capital to ring up and pay for their own groceries. Why did people invent a technology to eliminate people working in retail when billions of the people on the planet would be pleased to ring up your groceries? This labor-saving innovation was induced by distortions in the international market for labor.

Although something of an aside from labor projections, this is an important point, because one objection raised to allowing temporary labor mobility is that it creates "distortions" in the industries that survive on "cheap labor." The further argument is that if importing labor were impossible, then industries would not move abroad but would survive by inducing innovations that reduce labor demand and substitute capital for labor. For instance, Martin (2004) tells the story of tomatoes in California and, to my mind, gets the real point exactly backward. In the 1960s, as part of the *Bracero* program of allowing temporary migrant labor, tomatoes in California were picked almost entirely by seasonal migrants. When this program ended in the mid-1960s, farmers claimed the tomato industry would leave California. But by a combination of applying science to develop tomatoes whose shape and skin were more conducive to mechanization and developing a machine harvester, the California industry survived and even thrived—Martin emphasizes that it produces five times more tomatoes today than in the 1960s. But from an economist's point of view, what is the "distortion"—allowing seasonal workers (that is, more open labor markets across borders) or the induced-labor-demand-reducing technological change from enforcing a restriction that willing employers and willing workers could not make a contract?

Any economist, when presented with the same scenario with trade in goods, would be able to give an easy answer—if an industry invents a new technology to displace an imported intermediate input because the price of the input is driven up by border restrictions like tariffs or quotas, this innovation is a *response* to a distortion, not that the lack of a tariff to induce that innovation would be a "distortion." From a global viewpoint, highly skilled labor devoted to research and development to reduce demand for labor (for example, machine-harvestable tomatoes, lawn mowers, ATMs, self-checkout at retail stores, robots that vacuum, pre-peeled carrots) is an inefficiency that is the result of the massive "distortion" in global labor markets.[14] Because about the only thing known yet about "pro-poor" growth is that it is labor intensive, there is obviously a massive contradiction between rich countries pushing "pro-poor" growth via their rhetoric about development assistance while at the same time promoting massively anti-pro-poor technological change via their policies toward labor mobility.

Conclusion

The four forces for greater labor mobility across borders have been growing and will continue to grow:

—The gaps between what the same worker can make in one country versus another are higher than they have ever been in history—much higher than the wage differentials that drove the mass migrations of the nineteenth century.

—Demographic destinies will increase the gap in the relative supplies of young workers.

—The globalization of everything but labor has both reduced the costs and made the idea of mobility more acceptable.

—The continued expansion of jobs in low-skill, hard-core nontradable service industries in rich countries creates "pull" pressures.

---

14. This "distortion" perhaps changes the relative unskilled or skilled real wages in a country and hence may have positive effects for some people (the unskilled in the United States) and negative for others (unskilled elsewhere)—but then again, so do nearly all economic distortions.

2

The Fifth Irresistible Force: Ghosts and Zombies

The fifth force that creates increased pressures for labor mobility is rapid and massive shifts in the desired populations of various countries. In short, the current international economic system ignores the variability over time of the *desired* populations of nation-states by insisting on the mostly historically arbitrary but fixed borders of the current sovereign nation-states. This lack of labor mobility accounts for the dramatically poor economic performances that have been witnessed and is an obvious potential force for greater labor mobility. To be blunt, there is a significant possibility that millions, perhaps hundreds of millions, of people are living in nation-states that because of geographic and technological "shocks" to their economies have little or no possibility of sustaining their current populations (much less their projected future populations) with anything like decent standards of living.

This chapter first develops a bit of a framework for analyzing the variability in desired populations and then presents three pieces of empirical evidence that suggest that variability in desired populations is in fact quite large.[1] This fifth force is

1. This chapter draws heavily on my recent paper "Boom Towns and Ghost Countries: Geography, Agglomeration, and Population Mobility" (Pritchett 2004a).

43

discussed here in a separate chapter because while the other four forces are well known, this aspect has been a neglected part of the discussion and requires new evidence with some elaboration.

What Is the "Desired" Population of a Region?

The notion of the "perfect mobility" equilibrium or "unconstrained desired" population of a given geographic region is easy to define: "Given the current and expected future economic (policy, institutional, technological) and political and geographic circumstances, how many people would live in a given spatial territory in the long run if there were perfect mobility?" One could define the "optimal" population as the "unconstrained desired population with the best possible policies and institutions" (which does not assume that these "best possible" policies or institutions are homogenous across countries). This distinction is important because the "unconstrained desired" population of a region could change very fast (say, due to a civil war or disastrous economic policies), even though the "optimal" population has not changed. In this case, the obvious solution is to stick to "fix policies" or "resolve the conflict" so that the desired and optimal populations move closer. But technological shifts in the world economy can change the optimal populations—even with the best possible policies and institutions. For instance, once sea transport was possible, the (relative, or perhaps absolute) optimal population of regions that thrived on overland commerce declined and those near the coast increased.

Changes in desired populations do not create many pressures for labor mobility if they are small or very gradual. Changes in desired populations might be small or gradual if either (1) the economic fundamentals of the desired population do not change or (2) the mobility of goods or other factors (capital, trade) can compensate for shifts in region-specific labor demand. Labor mobility is not a big deal for Antarctica because no substantial human populations ever moved there; its attractiveness for human populations has not *changed*. But the classic counterexample is a regional gold rush—first, people do not want to be there; then gold is discovered, and many people want to be there; and then, when the gold is mined out, people want to leave. The existence of "ghost towns" even in prospering countries—places that were once booming and attracting migration that subsequently declined and even disappeared—suggest that there is variability to optimal populations.[2]

---

2. For me, the origin of some of this thinking is that I grew up near Idaho City, which was once a thriving frontier town (the largest in the Idaho territory) and had a population in 2000 of only 458. Why? Simple. There used to be gold in the river nearby, and now there is not any commercially exploitable gold.

But even if there are regional shocks, there might not be large variations in the desired population if the mobility of other factors can compensate. Suppose a region attracts population because it relies on one type of economic activity and then some natural or economic shock makes that activity no longer viable. There is no longer any reason for people to be *there* as opposed to any other place—but they are there. One possibility is that new activities are created and resources (capital) flow to that place and people sustain roughly their same living standards but change their activities. Certainly, in the story of many of the major cities of the world, the original reason for the city's location has long since ceased to be relevant (for example, fortification, transport linkages) but the city continues to thrive. Yet there are two other possibilities. One is that new resources do not flow in and the optimal population falls and people leave. The other possibility is that the optimal population falls, perhaps dramatically, but people are not allowed to leave for more attractive locations due to barriers to labor mobility, and hence all the adjustment to the variability in the optimal population of regions is forced onto real wages and living standards.

Suppose that a realistic feature of a model of the international or interregional economy are region-specific "shocks" that produce, even after all accommodating changes in capital stocks and goods, large persistent changes in regional labor demand. The simplest possible "supply–demand" diagram illustrates the possibilities.

If there are region-specific shocks to long-run labor demand and population mobility is allowed, then the regional supply of labor is elastic in the long run. In this case, one should observe large variability across regions in the growth rates of populations and relatively small variability in the interregional growth of real wages. In this case, large negative region-specific shocks to labor demand can create "ghosts"—regions that consistently lose population (either absolutely or just relatively) (figure 2-1).

If there are region-specific shocks to labor demand but population mobility is restricted and hence the regional supply of labor is inelastic, then the forces will be accommodated with large variability in the growth of wages (and incomes) across regions but relatively small variability in populations.

The consequence of a distribution of large region-specific changes in labor demand and restrictions on labor mobility is that there will be regions that experience large, persistent, positive shocks to labor demand and become boom towns. But there are also geographic regions that will experience large, persistent, negative shocks. Because desired (and optimal) populations can fall much faster than the actual population, this will create situations in which the *actual* population will vastly exceed its new "desired" level:

Figure 2-1. *How Changes in the Demand for Labor Cause Pressures for Labor Mobility*

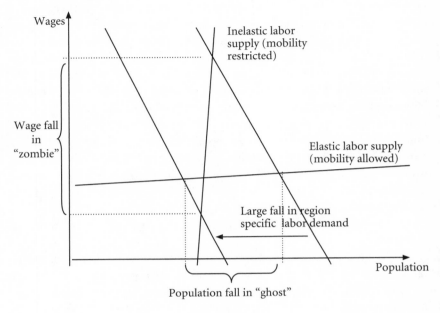

—If the negative shock is large enough and population movements are allowed, these regions will become actual ghosts.

—If the negative shock is large and other regions prevent labor mobility, then potential ghost countries become unrealized ghosts or "zombie" countries (zombies are the living dead) because nothing, besides out-migration, can prevent an extended and permanent fall in wages.

There are three sources of evidence, which together suggest that there are typically large shifts in the desired populations of regions. Though it is extremely difficult to separate out which of these are shifts in just an "unconstrained desired" population (due to remediable factors like policies, or, optimistically, institutions) and which are shifts in "optimal" populations, there is some evidence from comparing regions of countries (which share many policies and institutions) that some large fraction of the shifts in *desired* populations are also shifts in *optimal* population. These shifts in desired population are accommodated differently depending on the conditions for labor mobility. The three empirical examples are (1) regions of the United States, (2) comparisons of within-country versus cross-country variability of population and output per person growth rates, and (3) population versus output variability in history.

One important point, which I stress throughout this chapter, is this decomposition into changes in desired populations stemming from various underlying causes. There are changes in desired populations that are due to differences in income or income growth attributable to policies, politics, or institutions; and these changes are potentially remediable—quickly. Not every example of economic decline is an example in which population mobility is necessarily an important factor in the solution; it is plausible that a country's desired population is low, and pressures for outward labor movement are high, because the country is badly governed (for example, Zaire) or because of a macroeconomic crisis (for example, Argentina in 2000). Then fixing the problem at the source is obviously a much more attractive policy than allowing labor mobility. However, here I want to stress that there are determinants of long-run demand that are beyond the control of policies (or even "institutions," about which there is a debate on how much these can be purposively altered). It is perfectly plausible that, even with the best policies and institutions, a region can see its desired population fall by 50 percent or more due to economic forces—shifts in product demand, agglomeration, transport costs—interacting with the region's geographic features, and hence the desired population has fallen because the *optimal* population has fallen. This is a much more difficult issue to address.

Evidence of Shifts in Desired Populations: Regional Populations in the United States

A large country like the United States provides a good laboratory for examining changes in optimal populations. People are completely free to move, so regions tend toward their "unconstrained desired" population. Within a large country like the United States, "policies" and "institutions" are held roughly, though obviously not completely, equal. All U.S. regions have the same monetary policy, the same trade policy, roughly the same legal framework,[3] and similar politics. Nevertheless, U.S. states have had very different rates of population growth—a point that is returned to in the next subsection.

3. These are not, of course, precisely equal, as Louisiana has a "French" style legal system while all others have an Anglo civil law tradition, and some states are traditionally Democratic while others are traditionally Republican. But the differences are small compared with other regions (for instance, India, in which some states have had communist parties, other states have had more conservative parties, and still others have experienced quite personalized policies with state-specific parties organized around a single individual).

But state-level data understate the degree of labor mobility. If one moves from the state down to the county level, one finds counties that were essentially depopulated over the sixty years from 1930 to 1990. For instance, Slope County, North Dakota, saw its population fall from 4,150 to only 907; Smith County, Kansas, from 13,545 to 5,078; Huerfano County, Colorado, from 17,062 to 6,009; and McDowell County, West Virginia, from 90,479 to 35,233.

These are not isolated examples. Even though the United States overall more than doubled its population from 1930 to 1990, this growth was far from uniform. An instructive exercise is to assemble groups of counties that may cut across state boundaries but are *contiguous* and that are a shape such that it is at least conceivable that, had history been different, a plausibly shaped country could have been formed with these boundaries. That is, while we deliberately gerrymandered the areas to include population-losing counties, we did not simply "cut out" cities or make dramatic detours to include this or exclude that county.

I have assembled five regions of the United States, which, since I created them, I will name: *Texaklahoma* (Northwest Texas and Oklahoma), *Heartland* (parts of Iowa, Missouri, Kansas, and Nebraska), *Deep South* (parts of Arkansas, Mississippi, and Alabama), *Pennsylvania Coal* and *Great Plains North* (parts of Kansas and South Dakota). Even with the constraint of contiguity and (mostly) convexity, one can assemble large territories that have seen substantial *absolute* population decline. The Great Plains North is a territory larger than the United Kingdom, and its population declined 28 percent from 1930 to 1990. Its current population is only a bit more than a third the population it would have been if its population growth had been at the rate of natural increase. The Texaklahoma region is bigger than Bangladesh and is now only 31 percent the population size it would have been in the absence of outmigration. I use a few counties in the coal-producing region of Pennsylvania to illustrate that not all these declines are due to the decline of rural and agricultural populations—natural resource shocks also play a role (table 2-1).

The maps of these regions tell the story. Figures 2-2 through 2-5 show the county-by-county populations of the states that contain four of the regions described above. The shades of gray in the figures show counties that, over the course of sixty years in which the population of the United States doubled, saw their populations fall in absolute terms. The shading is by the absolute (not percentage) fall in population: Counties in dark gray lost more than 10,000; medium gray, 5,000 to 10,000; and light gray, 5,000 to 0. Areas with no shading (plain white) had modest population gains (up to 10,000), while the striped counties gained more than 10,000 in population.

Table 2-1. *Population Change in Assembled Regions, 1930–90*[a]

U.S. region	Population, 1930 (thousands)	Population change, 1930–90 (percent)	Current population/ counterfactual at rate of natural increase	Region area (square miles)	Countries of smaller area, with examples (number)[b]	Area per capita income as percentage of national average
Texaklahoma	835.8	−36.8	0.31	58,403	117 (Nicaragua, Bangladesh)	92.2
Heartland	1,482.6	−34.0	0.33	59,708	117	85.2
Deep South	1,558.2	−27.9	0.36	36,284	96 (Jordan, Austria, Sri Lanka)	62.6
Pennsylvania Coal	1,182.9	−27.9	0.36	2,972	43 (Trinidad and Tobago, Mauritius)	84.5
Great Plains North	1,068.0	−27.7	0.36	100,920	128 (United Kingdom, Ghana, Ecuador)	85.4
All U.S.	123,202.6	101.9		3,536,278	100.0	

Source: Pritchett 2004a.

a. A region is a contiguous collection of counties cutting across state borders.

b. Total number of countries considered is 192.

I am stressing obvious facts about population movements when I point out three things. First, economic forces have led to the decline of certain activities—like farming in the Great Plains, cotton farming in the South, and coal mining in Pennsylvania—and that has led to a large population exodus, particularly from rural areas and small cities.

Second, the rural–urban movement has, almost by definition, tended to cause small decreases in population in a large geographic area and large increases in a few concentrated areas (the shaded counties usually contain a major metropolitan area). This means that geographic regions without sufficient economic force to attract a major city tend to lose population absolutely, while areas with an urban center have large shifts in population.

Third, even though there were large population losses, this was without huge losses in absolute or relative income. As seen in table 2-1, even regions with dramatically declining populations have stayed quite close to the average

Figure 2-2. *Changes in County Populations in the U.S. "Heartland"*
Region (Selected Counties of Iowa, Missouri, Nebraska, and Kansas)[a]

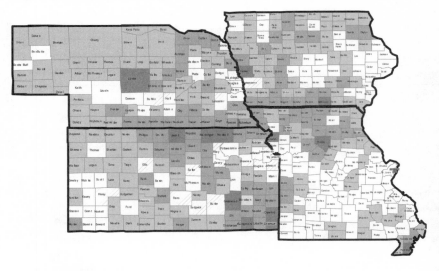

Source: Pritchett 2004a.
a. Dark gray: lost more than 10,000; medium gray: lost 5,000–10,000; light gray: lost 0–5,000; white: gained 0–10,000; striped: gained more than 10,000.

national income (with the exception of the Deep South). These regions and counties became ghosts, not zombies.

Regions within the United States serve as a thought experiment of what would happen in a fully "globalized" world—geographic units linked with fully integrated markets for land, capital, goods, *and* labor—and a globalized world with common policies and economic institutions at that. In such a world, one can expect that incomes would converge *in levels,* and, with the exception of the Deep South, incomes in these created regions are more than 84 percent of the national average. But one can ask—even with fully integrated markets with goods and capital—how much variability is there in "optimal populations"? The answer is "a lot." Though it may be the case that population movements were less than they would have been because capital flowed to these regions and goods were mobile, it is still the case that the population shifts within the United States are huge. In particular, they are vastly larger than the population shifts one sees across the often equally arbitrary boundaries of countries in the world today.

Figure 2-3. *Changes in County Populations in the U.S. "Deep South"*
Region (Selected Counties of Arkansas, Mississippi, and Alabama)[a]

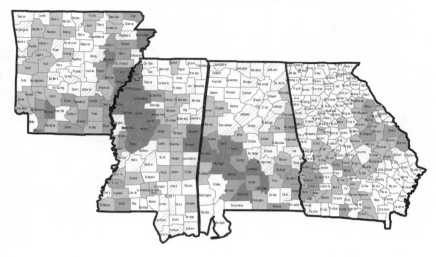

Source: Pritchett 2004a.
a. Dark gray: lost more than 10,000; medium gray: lost 5,000–10,000; light gray: lost 0–5,000; white: gained 0–10,000; striped: gained more than 10,000.

Adjustment of the Regions of Countries versus Countries in Output Growth and Population

The second illustration of the variability of desired populations is to show that the variability of the growth output per worker to the variability of the growth of population happens exactly as we would expect with large regional shocks. As illustrated in figure 2-1, with perfect labor mobility, workers and households will move in response to economic opportunities, and if there are large geographic shocks to regions that change desired populations (which, remember, is the combination of shocks and the shock not being fully accommodated by movements in other factors like capital or by trade) and the labor market is integrated, then the variability of the growth output per worker across regions should be relatively small, because regions with incipient rapid growth should gain population and regions with negative shocks lose population, while the variability of the growth rate of population should be large.

Figure 2-4. *Changes in County Populations in the U.S. "Pennsylvania Coal" Region (Selected Counties of Eastern Pennsylvania)*[a]

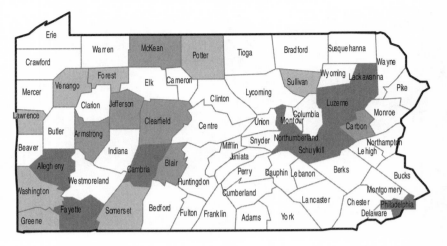

Source: Pritchett 2004a.
a. Dark gray: lost more than 10,000; medium gray: lost 5,000–10,000; light gray: lost 0–5,000; white: gained 0–10,000; striped: gained more than 10,000.

In contrast, if the world is segmented so labor and households cannot move *and* there are very different shocks to a geographic region's output potential, then the adjustment mechanism should be exactly the opposite. One would expect very little variability in the growth rates of population (because it is primarily determined by rates of natural increase) and enormous variability in the growth rate of output per person (or worker) as wages fall due to the geographic-specific productivity shock. This is the natural experiment that the postwar international system has run, and figures 2-6 and 2-7 show the results.

Because figures 2-6 and 2-7 are new, they require a bit of explanation, but, like all great art, it is worth it as this art embodies two features. First, the annual growth rates of output per capita and of population are on the vertical and horizontal axes. Though software packages that produce graphs rescale the axes independently so that one cannot visually compare the variability, in this case I have forced the axes to have exactly the same range. Second, I show the 90th and 10th percentile boxes of each variable, so that the two vertical lines contain 80 percent of the region's growth in population (because the rightmost line is the 90th percentile of population growth and the leftmost line is the 10th percentile). Similarly, for growth of output per capita, the top horizontal line

Figure 2-5. *Changes in County Population in the U.S. "Great Plains North" Region (Selected Counties of Nebraska and South Dakota)[a]*

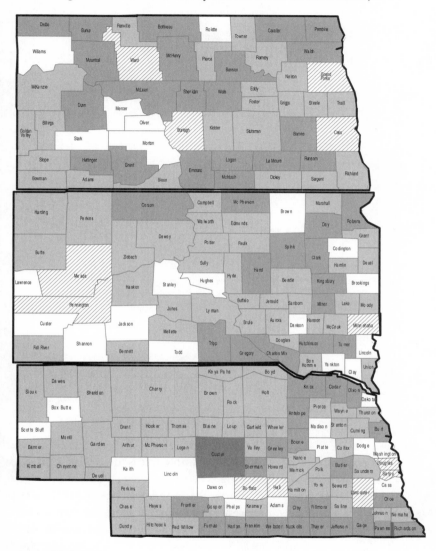

Source: Pritchett 2004a.
a. Dark gray: lost more than 10,000; medium gray: lost 5,000–10,000; light gray: lost 0–5,000; white: gained 0–10,000; striped: gained more than 10,000.

Figure 2-6. *Large Shocks, Accommodated with Population Growth in Large Countries, Per Capita Growth across Non-OECD Countries versus the United States, Japan, and Canada*

(Boxes at 90th/10th percentiles of each variable)

Growth of GDP (or income) per capita

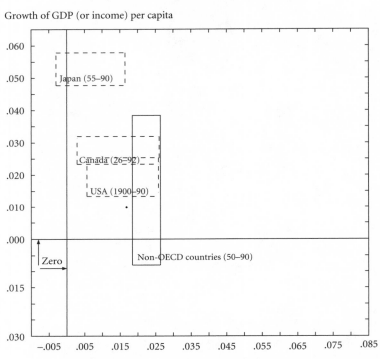

Growth of population less rate of natural increase

is the 90th percentile of growth while the bottom line is the 10th percentile. If regions have large regional shocks that lead to nearly equal output per capita growth but different population growth, then one would expect a long, skinny horizontal box. Conversely, if there are large regional shocks that are accommodated through wages and output, then there should be a tall, skinny vertical box. With small regional shocks, the boxes should be smaller because there is less to be accommodated either way.

These figures show exactly what we would expect with large changes in desired populations regionally but differences in restrictions on labor mobility—large countries have long, skinny horizontal boxes (nearly equal economic growth, differing population growth), while the other countries of the

Figure 2-7. *Large Shocks, Accommodated with Population Growth in Large Countries, Per Capita Growth across Non-OECD Countries versus European Countries*

(Boxes at 90th/10th percentiles of each variable)

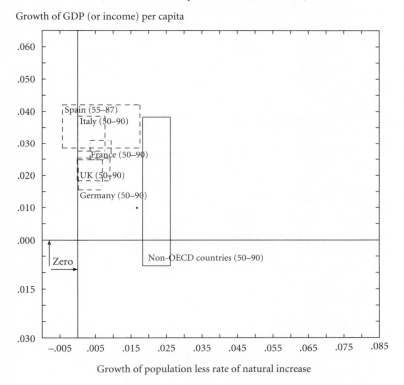

Growth of GDP (or income) per capita

Growth of population less rate of natural increase

world show tall, skinny boxes (very little population growth difference, huge differences in economic growth).[4] The standard deviation of growth rates of output per person across countries not belonging to the Organization for Economic Cooperation and Development (OECD) is 1.9 percent a year. This is five to six times larger than the typical standard deviation of output growth of regions within countries. In contrast, the standard deviation of the growth of population less the rate of natural increase—a proxy for the component of

4. This evidence alone of course does not resolve whether these variations across countries in labor demand are the result of "policies" (which presumably could be changed), "institutions" (which might be able to be changed), or geographic or technological shocks (which cannot be changed).

population growth due to mobility—is 0.40, which is half the population growth variability within regions of the United States, Canada, Japan, or Spain and about that of most European countries.

Adjusting to Shocks, Then versus Now

The nineteenth century was truly an "age of mass migration" (Hatton and Williamson 1998), because many of the "areas of recent settlement" had open borders with respect to immigrants (at least with certain ethnic and national origins). It was also an era of rapid reductions in transport costs and shifts toward freer trade in goods, open capital markets, and massive movements in capital—the first era of globalization. Hence, this period is an interesting example of the question: "How would we expect geographically specific shocks to be accommodated in a globalizing world?" Comparing Ireland to Bolivia highlights the obvious: that nearly all developing countries with negative shocks have seen their populations continue to expand rapidly, while when there was freer labor mobility in the international system, labor movements accommodated negative shocks (figures 2-8 and 2-9).

That is, during the entire period of Ireland's huge negative shock of the potato blight and its aftermath—a classic example of a region-specific shock that reduced desired, and likely optimal, population (just as the introduction

Figure 2-8. *Changes in Real Wages and Population during the Period of Accommodating the Shock of the Potato Famine and Its Aftermath in Ireland, 1810–1920*[a]

Relative to 1870=1

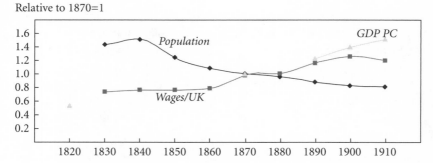

Sources: Maddison 2001 for population and GDP per capita; O'Rourke and Williamson 1999 for real wages.

a. Index of population, real unskilled urban wages, and GDP per capita, 1870–71.

Figure 2-9. *Changes in Real Wages and Population during the Period of Accommodating Negative Shocks in Bolivia, 1970–95*[a]

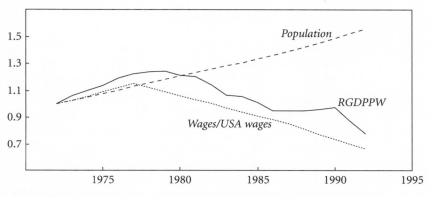

1972=1

Sources: Penn World Tables 6.0 for output and population; Rama and Arcetona 2002 for industrial wages.

a. Index of population, real industial wages relative to the United States, and GDP per capita, 1972 = 1.

of the potato, by lowering the cost of calories per hectare, had raised optimal population)—real wages in Ireland relative to the United Kingdom never fell and gross domestic product (GDP) per capita never fell.

In contrast, Bolivia had a clear negative shock as well, but one that occurred in a period in which there was little or no international labor mobility. So, rather than the shock being accommodated by changes in population while real wages of Bolivians remained constant (both in Bolivia and elsewhere), real wages in Bolivia fell spectacularly.

Implications for Labor Mobility

Zambia is a country with a clear narrative. In part, people moved to Zambia, and to a particular region of Zambia, because you could dig a hole in the ground and extract something valuable (copper).[5] Around that large hole in the ground, a city developed. Now, the world economy and technological

---

5. I ike the example of Zambia because as a schoolchild I visited the world's largest open pit copper mine, the Bingham Mine outside Salt Lake City. Since the price of copper has fallen, there have been hard times in the regions near the mine, and the mine has changed ownership three times as various corporations have gotten into dire financial straits.

conditions have changed such that it is likely the case that the profitability of digging copper out of the ground has been permanently reduced. Zambia is also landlocked, so exporting manufactures is probably not in the cards. Zambia is not particularly "overpopulated" in the absolute sense of land/labor ratios, but if Zambia were a region of a larger, integrated, geographic unit, then its population would likely be a small fraction of what it is today. The population of the Pennsylvania coal counties, where mining has shrunk as a viable economic activity, declined by 30 percent in absolute terms over sixty years. Zambia's population is *twice* what it was at its peak output per person. If we assume that Zambia's *optimal* population has fallen by as much as the regions in the United States—30 percent—then Zambia's current population is almost three times higher than its optimal population.[6] It is hard to see how anything other than large sustained migration is going to reverse that.

One should rightly hesitate to declare that any particular territory is simply incapable of supporting its current population at acceptable standards of living. But, conversely, simply maintaining a fiction because it is politically convenient for industrial countries is no better. I define potential "ghost" countries (which are all, given the lack of population mobility, zombies) as countries where (1) GDP per capita has fallen by more than 20 percent from peak to trough (where, for data purposes, the peak must come before 1990, so recent ghosts are ruled out), and (2) GDP per capita today remains less than 90 percent of peak GDP. This produces a list of thirty-three countries.

Of this list, I have no way of showing which countries are "geographic" ghosts and which are not. In particular, I have no way of knowing which of these are "policy and institutional" ghosts and which are "geographic" ghosts. That is, it could be that anticipated output fell because of disastrously bad politics or policies, which, if reversed, would cause the area to be enormously attractive—think of the boom Cuba is going to have when Fidel Castro is gone, for instance. To document which are geographic ghosts, I would have to specify and parameterize some particular model of location, which would require grappling with the thorny issues of increasing returns to scale and the like. Instead, I will do two calculations, which are *hypothetical,* and simply illustrate the consequences of the possibility that these countries are ghosts.

First, because output per person has fallen in all these countries (by definition), I ask the question: "*If* optimal population has received as large a neg-

---

6. Of course, this assumes that even with "best possible" policies and institutions, there is still a large shock to the desired population, which is impossible to prove, because Zambia has combined bad shocks with not the most sterling track record on the other dimensions.

ative shock relative to its peak in this country as it has in the counterfactual [see three options below], then what is the ratio of the postshock population to the current population?" The three counterfactual scenarios are "What if the population in country Y has fallen relative to its population at peak GDP per capita by as much as the actual population

—fell peak to trough in Ireland in the nineteenth century (53 percent)?"

—fell between 1930 and 1990 in three regions of the United States (Deep South, Great Plains North, Pennsylvania Coal) (28 percent)?"

—rose only as fast as the bottom 10th percentile of population growth in regions of the eight OECD countries in table 2-1 (0.01 percent a year)?"

This is obviously not "proof" of the changes in the desired populations of the countries, but just a matter of exploring the implications of plausible counterfactual scenarios. In all these regions, GDP per capita rose substantially while populations fell. In the countries, GDP per capita fell while populations rose. It is at least plausible that these simply represent different adjustments to similar-sized shocks to geographic-specific maximal incomes, pushing the adjustment either into wages and capital stocks or into population movement.

Second, I ask the question: If the elasticity of GDP per person with respect to population is negative 0.4, by how much would population have to fall in order to

—restore previous peak GDP per capita, or

—move GDP per capita to the level it would be had it grown at 2 percent a year since the peak (roughly the world average growth rate, hence just avoiding divergence)?

Table 2-2 shows ghosts that I believe are "hard-core" ghosts, in that they are *optimal* population ghosts, not just desired population ghosts, for three reasons (actually, to keep the technical terminology clear, these ghosts are currently embodied as zombies because of population restrictions but would be ghosts with labor mobility). First, the decline is more likely geographic than policy or institutional. Though none of these countries has terrific policies or institutions, they are not the Zaires of the world that have resource abundance but are political or institutional ghosts. Second, all these countries are landlocked, which makes the substitution into other industries more difficult. Third, they all have "small" populations (less than 20 million), which suggests that, in a locational equilibrium with population mobility, there might not be sufficient population for even one large city to serve as a growth pole, in which case the declines in desired population might be even more dramatic than those in the table because of the agglomeration effects.

Table 2-2. How Large Is the Ghosthood?a

| Country or region | Year of peak GDP per capita (GDPpc) | Ratio GDPpc-2000/GDPpc-peak | Current population | Ratios of the population to the current actual population if... | | | | |
| | | | | ...the shock was as large as the realized population changes in the following three cases: | | | ...the labor force fell to restore GDP per capita to X assuming an elasticity of output per person to population of –0.4 | |
				Ireland 48% fall from 1841 to 1926 (percent)	U.S. ghost regions 28% fall from 1930 to 1990 (percent)	OECD lagging regionsb (percent)	Previous peak GDP per capita 0.4 (percent)	GDP per capita implying 2% annual growth since peak (no divergence) 0.4 (percent)
Zambia	1964	0.59	10,089	18	25	35	36	14
CAF zone	1970	0.44	3,603	27	37	51	24	11
Niger	1963	0.50	10,832	17	23	32	29	11
Chad	1979	0.50	7,694	30	41	57	29	17
Rwanda	1981	0.75	8,508	33	45	63	55	30
Bolivia	1978	0.87	8,329	33	44	62	72	34
Romania	1986	0.74	22,435	54	74	103	54	34

Source: Author's calculations.

a. Potential hard-core ghosts.

b. Average of P10 of population growth (0.01 percent per annum growth).

CAF = African Financial Community Franc; GDP = gross domestic product; OECD = Organization for Economic Cooperation and Development.

Because I began with Zambia, let me use it to illustrate both the very simple way the five scenarios work and the results. Zambia's GDP per capita peaked in 1964 when its population was 3.5 million. Today, its GDP per capita is only 59 percent of the peak, and the population is 10 million. If Zambia's population had fallen from its 1964 level by as much as Ireland's actual population (48 percent), then its population today would be only 1.86 million—18 percent of its current level. If Zambia's population had fallen from its 1964 level by as much as population has fallen in three of the ghost regions in the United States (28 percent), then its population would only be 2.52 million—25 percent of its current level. If Zambia's population had grown at the 0.01 percent of the 10th percentile in population growth regions of the eight OECD countries, its population today would be about what it was in 1964, 3.52 million—but that is only 35 percent of its current level.

The two output scenarios provide similarly striking ratios. Under the simple assumptions made about population and output per person, population would have to fall to 14 percent of its current level to raise GDP per person to the level of a nondivergent trend. This is consistent with a negative shock roughly the magnitude of Ireland's. To raise output per person just to its previous peak, the populations would have to fall to 36 percent of their current levels.

I am aware of how striking these numbers are. But it is not implausible that the optimal population of the Sahel (for example, Niger, Chad) has fallen by as much as the optimal population of the Great Plains North counties of the United States. That is, there is nothing of any particular "Afro-pessimism" in this; this is not about the culture or politics of Africa any more than it is about the culture or politics of Iowa or North Dakota (which are quite good). If this is so, then, if population mobility were not constrained, three out of every four people would leave Niger, and this might only be enough to restore output to its level of 1963. With the simple assumed elasticities, Chad, just to return to its previous peak (1979) GDP per capita, would require that seven of every ten people leave.

Conclusion

One force for increased population mobility is that many countries in the world have experienced large negative shocks, such that, even with the best possible responses in policies and institutions, the optimal population has fallen significantly. In the current international system, these people are trapped. A helpful way of thinking about desired populations is the following: There are 10 million people in the Sahelian country of Niger; if there were globally free labor mobility and only 1 million lived in Niger now, how many people would move there? Though some people might say that this creates a case for more aid or freer trade, it is hard to believe that if people moved out of Kansas because farming was no longer an attractive opportunity, then the best that can be done for the people of Niger or Chad is that they get slightly more assistance and slightly better prices for the items they grow. The fifth irresistible force for labor mobility is changes over time in the optimal populations of regions as economic opportunities change.

3

Immovable Ideas: Myths and Truths

W hat stops the five massive, and mounting, pressures for movements of labor from resulting in even greater flows of people across borders? Ultimately, ideas do. However, the proximate cause that inhibits labor mobility is *coercion*. People with guns apply force to prevent people from crossing borders. People with guns force people to leave if discovered in a country without permission. The fact that this coercive force is (usually) exercised with domestic political legitimacy, restraint, or even prudence in rich countries should not mask the fact that it is coercion.[1] The threat or actual exercise of nation-state coercion prevents people from crossing borders to participate in ordinary economic transactions—like haircuts, buying food, and arranging home repairs—that are routine within countries and would be voluntary and mutually beneficial. In all the rich industrial countries, this coercion is under the complete control of a legitimate democratic state, which almost certainly faithfully, if crudely, represents in some way the preferences of its current citizens. Following that

1. The protections provided to asylum seekers before expulsion, for instance, generate costs and resentments that many asylum seekers are not "legitimate"—precisely because the coercion is so, appropriately, hedged about with protections.

chain of causes, the ultimate reason that there is not massively more mobility of labor across national borders is that the *citizens of the rich industrial world do not want it*. Standing firm against the irresistible economic forces for greater labor mobility are the immovable ideas of rich-country citizens, and this contrast between economic forces and ideas is what has led to the current policy deadlock.

This chapter first presents some estimates of the magnitude of the current flows and stocks of labor mobility to show that the flows are both made much lower and distorted by existing restrictions on migration and labor mobility. The chapter then reports on opinion survey information to document the obvious: that any *increase* in labor mobility or migration is decidedly unpopular in the rich industrial countries. The next two sections review the ideas that support and sustain the restrictions against the movement of persons, first a discussion of the ideas that underpin the moral legitimacy of restrictions and second the "self-interested" arguments against greater labor mobility.

The chapter concludes with an examination of why, in spite of the current resistance to increased labor mobility, this issue should be squarely on the development agenda. This chapter's review of the eight ideas that together create resistance to increases in movement across borders is not to suggest that it is impossible; rather, this chapter sets the stage for the following chapter, which examines how proposals for development-friendly increases in labor mobility can be made politically feasible. As documented in chapters 1 and 2, the problem is not a lack of economic benefits of labor mobility. There are large potential "gains from trade" from allowing people on both sides of the border to enter into voluntary and mutually beneficial contracts. Because the constraints on labor flows are ideas, not economics, the main challenge is not to generate proposals that produce economic gains (that is easy) but to produce proposals that are politically feasible in rich countries—while remaining development friendly.

The Magnitude and Structure of Current Migration

The five increased pressures for labor mobility have resulted in increasing flows of people across borders. Although the "irresistible forces" are actively resisted by policy, these have not been fully effective. Martin (2004) estimates that just five industrial countries (Canada, Germany, the Netherlands, the United Kingdom, and the United States) spend $17 billion annually on enforcement and caring for asylum seekers. Though this has obviously not been completely effective in preventing illegal flows, this coercive intervention of industrial-country governments does stop the flows of people across borders from being enormously higher than they could be with different policies—and distorts what limited movement that exists.

Estimating annual labor flows by type is a difficult exercise. Goldin and Beath (forthcoming) give one set of estimates of the world's flows of people, placed into various categories based on visa/legal category, expected duration of stay, and skill category. Their estimate of the total annual global *flow* of people (excluding tourism and very-short-term visits) is about 11.1 million. Of these, only 3.5 million are "low-skill expatriates." Moreover, the main recipients of these are not industrial countries but the Gulf States (for example, Saudi Arabia, Kuwait, and the United Arab Emirates) or richer South East Asian countries (for example, Malaysia). The main flows to the industrial countries are high-skill expatriates, permanent settlers at the top end of skill distribution, or asylum seekers and undocumented migrants.

Table 3-1 uses recent data from the Organization for Economic Cooperation and Development (OECD) to produce estimates of the *stock* of the foreign born in OECD countries—dividing people's national origin into people born in developing and rich industrial OECD member countries.[2] We see that the total stock of people living in the rich industrial countries (unfortunately excluding Germany, whose data are not comparable) is 50 million, or about 7 percent of the population—but this falls to only 5 percent if one excludes the United States, which has more than half this total (28.4 million of the 50 million).

The question arises: "How low is the observed current flow or stock relative to the demand for labor mobility created by the pressures documented in the previous chapters?" The problem is that it is very difficult to answer this question without appearing foolish. That is, if one calculates how much higher labor mobility would be with completely open borders, this leaves one open to ridicule as naive or utopian (or dystopian, depending on one's view). Most policy discussions are "incrementalist" and ask only about the consequences of small(ish) policy changes—as, in chapter 1, the comparison of the gains from the incremental trade liberalization in the Doha round negotiations to the global free movement of labor seem facetious. However, because the current magnitude of migration is a balance of forces that includes coercion, one does want some sense of the magnitude of the total "excess demand" for labor mobility that is being choked off by the exercise of compulsion. Again, this is not to say that the flows "open borders" would produce

2. For these purposes, Mexico and South Korea, which are recent entries into the OECD club, are classified as "non-OECD."

Table 3-1. *Foreign-Born Population of Rich Industrial OECD Countries from Developing Countries*

Country	Total population (millions)	Population from developing countries (millions)	Percent of total population	Top five source countries (percent of total)	Top five source countries
Australia	18.1	2.2	12.0	35.2	Vietnam, China, Philippines, India, unknown
Canada	29.6	3.3	11.2	29.6	China, India, Hong Kong, Philippines, Vietnam
New Zealand	3.6	0.3	9.0	37.2	Samoa, China, South Africa, Fiji, India
United States	281.4	28.4	10.1	45.2	Mexico, Philippines, Puerto Rico, India, China
Total— traditional immigration	332.8	34.2	10.3		
Austria	8.0	0.6	7.9	54.5	Former Yugoslavia–Serbia and Montenegro, Former Yugoslavia–Bosnia and Herzegovina, Turkey, Romania, Former Yugoslavia-Croatia
Belgium	10.3	0.4	4.3	45.2	Morocco, Turkey, Congo, Dem. Rep., Former Yugoslavia–Serbia and Montenegro, Algeria
Switzerland	7.3	1.0	13.1	50.1	Former Yugoslavia–Serbia and Montenegro, Turkey, Former Yugoslavia–Bosnia and Herzegovina, unknown
Denmark	5.4	0.2	4.5	31.7	Turkey, Iraq, Former Yugoslavia–Bosnia and Herzegovina, Lebanon, unknown
Spain	40.8	1.5	3.7	44.2	Morocco, Ecuador, Colombia, Argentia, Venezuela
Finland	5.2	0.1	1.7	53.1	Former USSR, Former Yugoslavia–Serbia and Montenegro, Somalia, unknown
France	58.5	3.7	6.4	20.4	Algeria, Morocco, Tunisia, Turkey, Vietnam

United Kingdom	58.8	3.0	5.1	30.1	India, Pakistan, Bangladesh, Jamaica, South Africa
Greece	10.9	0.9	8.2	65.7	Albania, Turkey, Former USSR, Bulgaria
Ireland	3.9	0.1	2.0	31.7	Nigeria, South Africa, Romania, China, Philippines
Luxembourg	0.4	0.0	5.8	45.3	Former Yugoslavia–Serbia and Montenegro, Cape Verde, United Kingdom, Former Yugoslavia–Bosnia and Herzegovina
Netherlands	16.0	1.2	7.6	48.6	Suriname, Turkey, Indonesia, Morocco, Netherlands Antilles
Norway	4.6	0.2	4.1	26.6	Iraq, Pakistan, Former Yugoslavia–Serbia and Montenegro, Former Yugoslavia–Bosnia and Herzegovina, Vietnam
Portugal	10.4	0.5	4.5	62.8	Angola, Mozambique, Brazil, Cape Verde, Venezuela
Sweden	9.0	0.6	6.7	36.2	Former Yugoslavia–Serbia and Montenegro, Iraq, Former Yugoslavia–Bosnia and Herzegovina, Iran, Turkey
Total, Western Europe	249.4	14.1	5.6		
Japan	127	1.2	1.0	69.6	North Korea, South Korea, China, Brazil, Philippines
Total, rich industrial	709.1	49.5	7.0		
Total, less United States	427.7	21.1	4.9		

Source: Organization for Economic Cooperation and Development (OECD) data. Mexico, Turkey, and South Korea are classified as "developing" even though they are OECD countries. Because the data from Germany were insufficiently comparable, it was excluded.

are either desirable or feasible (in fact, the main argument of this chapter is that they are *not* politically feasible). But let me give five illustrations that suggest the irresistible economic forces documented in chapters 1 and 2 would produce, if unchecked, a cross-national labor mobility factor several multiples higher than the presently observed flows.

First, there are rich countries that, for a variety of reasons, do have enormously larger stocks of the foreign born than the rich industrial countries. The Gulf States, some city states (for example, Singapore), and Israel all have fractions of the foreign born that are above a quarter of their population. As a way of illustrating excess demand for labor movement, certainly the rich countries—if they chose to allow it—could attract enough immigrants to match the same fraction of the foreign born as Saudi Arabia. This would imply more than tripling the developing-country-born populations in the OECD from 49 million to 183 million. Similarly, it is hard to believe that OECD countries like France and Canada could not, if they chose, attract the same fraction of migrants as Singapore—which would imply almost *quintupling* the stock from 49 million to about 240 million. Of course, these are underestimates, because Saudi Arabia and Singapore do not have "open borders" or allow foreigners access to their labor market, but rather strictly limit work opportunities (more on this point below) (figure 3-1).

A second crude calculation of excess demand is to compare current *out*-migration rates to those in the first historical period of globalization. Thus, Goldin and Beath (forthcoming) estimate that about 8.5 million people move each year (excluding "students," "visa-free migrants," and "high-skill expatriates" from the total) as a crude (over)estimate of the total population movement from developing countries. This suggests that only 1.6 people *per thousand* move across borders in any given year. As chapter 1 documented, nearly all the economic pressures for mobility were *lower* in the first globalization period (1870–1910), but barriers were absent between immigrant-sending European countries and -receiving countries. How do current net out-migration rates compare with the flows out of sending European countries in the first period of globalization? During the first stage of globalization, 1870 to 1910, migration rates from European sending countries were much higher—3.2 per 1,000 in Denmark, 5 in Sweden, 8.5 in Italy, and more than 13 in Ireland. Even in what was then the world's leading economy, the United Kingdom, the net emigration rate was 2.7 per 1,000.

If one were to extrapolate these historical rates to the developing world, they would result in annual flows ranging from twice as high (at Denmark's rate) to five times as high (at Italy's rate) to more than eight times as high if

Figure 3-1. *The Foreign-Born Population as a Proportion of the Total Population*

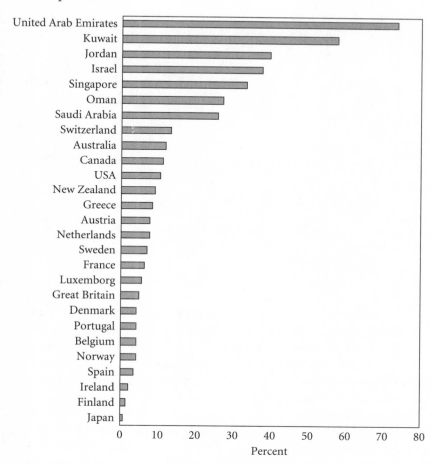

Sources: OECD 2004; UN Department of Economic and Social Affairs 2002.

the developing world on average had the out-migration rates observed in Ireland (table 3-2). This is not to say that these rates are "feasible," because at Italy's historical out-migration rate, this would imply annual *flows* of 45 million, which is nearly equal to the entire *stock* of developing-country foreign-born people in rich industrial countries today (49 million). This just illustrates that labor mobility is likely lower than it could be by a factor of between two and five, because it is constrained by host-country policies.

Table 3-2. *Emigration Rates from the Developing World Compared with Flows from European Countries in the Late Nineteenth Century[a]*

Hypothetical annual flow if the developing world had same emigration rate as the historical flow of	Millions of people	Historical flows, per thousand 1870–1910
United Kingdom	14.0	2.67
Denmark	16.8	3.20
Sweden	26.1	4.99
Norway	32.7	6.24
Italy	44.7	8.54
Ireland	69.9	13.35

Sources: Goldin and Beath forthcoming (estimates of current flow) and table 1-3 (historical net emigration rates).

a. The estimated current flow of developing-world emigrants is 8.5 million, with 1.62 emigrants per 1,000 population.

Third, there is something of an interesting "natural experiment" in the Caribbean region, for some islands became independent countries while others did not. Residents of Puerto Rico or the U.S. Virgin Islands are U.S. citizens and hence can freely move to the United States. Similarly, residents of the Netherlands Antilles can freely move to the Netherlands. Though obviously one does not want to extrapolate from small Caribbean islands to world migration, there are other nearby countries—often with a similar history, economy, and language—that are independent countries and hence face restricted immigration. If one compares the figures, one finds the obvious: that the ratio of the population in the United States or the Netherlands compared with the population resident on the islands is very high—52 percent for the U.S. Virgin Islands, 37 percent for Puerto Rico and the Netherlands Antilles—when mobility is unconstrained. This is true even though (no doubt in part due to migration) the ratio of gross domestic product (GDP) per capita is about 40 percent that of the larger country. In contrast, Dominicans in the United States are only 7.8 percent of those resident in the Dominican Republic—even though GDP per capita is only 16 percent as high as that of the United States. Haiti (granted, with a different history, languages, cultural ties, and so on) only has 5.3 percent as many Haitians living in the United States as resident in Haiti, while GDP per capita is only 4 percent that of the United States (and has

Table 3-3. *Territories' Fraction of the Population in the "Home" Country Compared with That in Independent Countries*

Country or territory	Resident population (thousands)	Foreign born in United States[a]	Single destination country/ resident population (percent)	GDP per capita (percent)	Ratio (percent)
Puerto Rico	3,917	1,440	36.8	17,700	44.1
Netherlands Antilles	220	83	37.7	11,400	38.6
Virgin Islands	109	57	52.5	17,200	42.9
Dominican Republic	8,950	701	7.8	6,300	15.7
Haiti	8,122	427	5.3	1,500	3.7
Jamaica	2,732	568	20.8	4,100	10.2

Sources: Organization for Economic Cooperation and Development data for foreign born in the United States or Netherlands. *CIA Factbook* for populations and purchasing power parity gross domestic product (GDP) per capita for territories and countries.

a. Or Netherlands for Netherlands Antilles.

few immediate prospects for improvement). It is difficult to believe that if there were freer migration these emigration ratios would not look much more similar across the Caribbean countries (table 3-3).[3]

Fourth, beginning in 1995, the United States legislated a "diversity visa" lottery for permanent residency. In the past five years, more than 10 million people a year have applied for the 50,000 available visas. Interestingly, only about half the winners actually use the visa (conditions demand that the winner move to the United States almost immediately). But with that uptake rate, this suggests that, in any given year, at least 5 million people are willing to move to the United States immediately. Because they are allowed to bring families, this may imply an "excess demand" from 5 million (no families) to 20 million (average of four per family) people *per year,* and this just to the United States. The upper number is approximately *twice* as large as the total flow from developing countries to *all* countries for *all* reasons (8.5 million). I suspect that the United States is not a uniquely attractive country and that a similar program in France, Sweden, Germany, or Australia would reveal sim-

3. It is also interesting to note that even with free labor mobility (education adjusted) wage gaps do not close entirely. This is consistent with a view that there are many factors entering into locational decisions other than pure wage gaps and that many people prefer to live where they were born and raised, near their extended family, and the like.

ilarly large "excess demand" for residency. If we take 20 million and scale up by the U.S. share of industrial-country population (on the crude, but perhaps accurate, assumption that all OECD countries are equally attractive), then the "revealed demand" of people willing to move immediately for an offer of permanent residence in an OECD country is 50 million a year—at least five times the annual flow and equal to the total current stock of developing-country population in OECD countries.[4]

Fifth, the World Bank's *World Development Report* on youth (World Bank 2006) commissioned a survey that asked young people (age fifteen to twenty-four years) the question "If it were possible for you legally to move to another country to work, would you?" Compared with the numbers on actual migration (which are on the order of 2 to 3 per 1,000 population) the numbers are astounding. The answer options were "not move," "try it out," "move temporarily," and "move permanently." Taking just the firmly expressed desire (that is, leaving out "try it out"), the survey suggests that 73 percent of Bangladeshi males, 69 percent of Romanian males, 64 percent of Albanian males, and 67 percent of Tajik males would like to move to work in another country. Even in Malaysia, which is both middle income and growing rapidly, 20.6 percent of young men would like to move to work.

Sixth, if one still doubted that there was a huge "excess demand" for access to the labor markets of rich countries, the media are increasingly reporting stories of the harrowing, and often tragic, risks that people are willing to take to enter rich countries. Because legal entry is restricted to levels far below the demand for entry at existing gaps in earnings, people are willing to undertake journeys of great physical hardship, danger, and risk just for the chance of employment in a rich-country labor market. Any suggestion that—because of cultural differences, family ties, or the attraction of the familiar—people do not really want to move and that these wage gaps do not create enormous pressures for workers to move is belied by the day-to-day reality of risk, hardship, and danger at the borders.

Legal barriers to labor mobility do more than reduce the totals; they also distort labor flows in a range of undesirable ways. When an otherwise ordinary transaction is made illegal, it creates an opportunity for criminal elements to become involved. For instance, when Prohibition in the United States made alcoholic drinks illegal, it created space for organized crime to dominate the trade in alcoholic beverages. When movement of people is made illegal, then criminal elements become involved, and those who move

4. Although this crude calculation may overstate the total demand, permanent residence in the United States and in other OECD countries are close substitutes.

often leave themselves at their mercy. Moreover, the whole otherwise ordinary process of people moving to seek out their best opportunity becomes tainted with illegality—perfectly ordinary job placement processes are called "labor smuggling." Moreover, because they are illegal, the workers themselves suffer because they feel they have little or no recourse and hence are abused by employers and intermediaries. But just as organized crime has intrinsically nothing to do with having a cocktail, these are not features of labor movements across national borders; these abuses and criminality are *not* intrinsic to cross-border labor flows but rather are the side effects of making these movements illegal.

One hesitates to belabor the obvious, but it is important to explode any reassuring myths that attempt to cover the fact that enormous pent-up pressures for labor mobility are held in check by coercion, plain and simple. This is not to deny that there are powerful forces keeping people in place, because people have many noneconomic motivations—family, history, language, culture, traditions, a sense of social belonging. No one is suggesting that people, by and large, would not prefer to stay in their "home" location—they do. The high emigration rate of Sweden in the age of unlimited migration was 5 per 1,000 population. Nor is anyone suggesting that all or most labor mobility is intended as permanent migration. But tens of millions of people would be willing to take advantage of the opportunity to work in a rich country—even if only under stringent conditions that did not give them either access to the "labor market" of the host country or hope of acquiring citizenship.

Increased Migration Is Unpopular in Industrial Countries

The International Social Survey Program asked people in many different countries around the world if they were in favor of or against higher levels of immigration. Table 3-4 reports the results in four regions: migration-receiving Western Europe, Japan, traditional migration-receiving countries, and traditional migration-sending countries. Though these data are dated, they are the best cross-nationally comparable data available.

In Western Europe, proposals to increase levels of immigration were dramatically unpopular. The proportion of the population that favored *reducing* immigration was more than three-quarters in Germany and Italy, and more than 60 percent in the United Kingdom, the Netherlands, Sweden, and Norway. Moreover, nearly all those who do not want migration reduced want it to remain the same. In no country in receiving Western Europe was the support for *any* increase in immigration (either "a little" or "a lot") higher than 10 percent. In Japan, a country where migration had

Table 3-4. *Public Views on Immigration*

Country or region	"Should immigration . . ." (percentages of those expressing an opinion)			
	Be reduced either "a lot" or "a little"	Remain the same	Increase either "a lot" or "a little"[a]	Fraction saying "let anyone come"[b]
Receiving Western Europe				
West Germany	77.58	19.62	2.82	13.8
Italy	75.6	20.84	3.55	
Austria	56.14	39.92	3.96	
United Kingdom	68.22	27.65	4.12	
Netherlands	61.51	33.02	5.47	
Sweden	69.77	23.52	6.71	8.4
Norway	63.2	29.37	7.43	4.9
Spain	40.07	51.48	8.44	14.6
Japan	42.27	42.06	15.68	4.2
Traditional recipient countries				
United States	65.78	26.17	8.05	5.1
New Zealand	62.62	25.78	11.58	
Canada	42.07	37.33	20.61	
Traditional sending countries				
Ireland	21.62	59.27	19.1	
Philippines	61.74	26.8	11.47	

Source: Mayda 2002, based on International Social Survey Program, national identity module, 1995.
a. Sorted in ascending order by fraction in favor of "increasing" within regions.
b. From World Values Survey data on "open borders."

been quite low, almost 16 percent of the population favored some increase in immigration—but even there, almost three times as many wanted immigration reduced.

In the United States and New Zealand, countries that were populated primarily by migration, opposition to increases in migration was also widespread. Of course, this is the context of the fact that actual immigration was increasing, a point we return to below. Of all the industrial countries, Canada emerges as the most favorably disposed to increased immigration. This means that in Canada *one in five* people favored increasing migration and only 42 percent favored reducing migration. So, at least in this particular survey as of 1995, in the industrial country that was the most "migrant friendly," "only" twice as many people wanted to *reduce* the level of migration as wanted it increased.

It is not as if those in favor of reducing migration are counterbalanced by a large group that opposes restrictions on immigration and wants increased mobility. In nearly every instance, those who want reductions in migration outnumber those who want it by ten to one. The World Values Survey reports that only a tiny fraction of the population (between 4 and 14 percent) agreed with the statement that their country should "let anyone come" (see table 3-5 below).

Not surprisingly, the views of governments reflect the views of the voters. In the UN *International Migration Report 2002* (UN Department of Economic and Social Affairs 2002), the policy stances of governments were reviewed. Of forty-eight "more developed" country governments, only two thought the level of immigration was "too low," while fourteen thought it was "too high" and thirty-two satisfactory. Of these same forty-eight "more developed" countries, twenty-one reported undertaking policies to lower immigration while again only two had policies to raise the level of immigration.

Of course, some of the opposition to increased immigration is a response to the fact that there were large *increases* in immigration in many countries in

Table 3-5. *Support for Aid to Immigrants' Home Countries in Countries Where Immigration Is Opposed*

Country	Fraction "in favor" of aid	Fraction saying "too little" effort for poverty in less developed countries	Fraction saying "let anyone come"
West Germany	83.0	65.2	13.8
Spain	85.1	64.9	14.6
United States	55.5	62.4	5.1
Japan	90.4	42.8	4.2
Australia	74.7	63.5	4.6
Norway	81.6	51.6	4.9
Sweden	83.9	51.6	8.4

Source: World Values Survey, third wave (1995–97). For column 1, "Some people favor, and others are against, having this country provide economic aid to poorer countries. Are you personally . . ." the options were "very much for," "for to some extent," "somewhat against," and "very much against," and were reported as either "very much" or "to some extent" for. Column 2, "In some economically less developed countries, many people are living in poverty. Do you think that what the other countries of the world are doing to help them is about right, too much or too little?" was reported as "too little." Column 3, "How about people from other countries coming here to work? Which of the following do you think the government should do?" was reported as "Let anyone come who wants to."

the 1990s—although from a very low base.[5] That is, in spite of the general unpopularity of movements of labor and population, they are occurring and increasing. But because ideas are the key constraint to more development-friendly policies toward labor mobility, the key issue is not demonstrating the potential gains to movers but designing policies that reflect the generation of new ideas for alleviating the *political* constraints.

However, understanding these political constraints created by ideas requires examining the ideas that sustain opposition to labor mobility in the rich industrial countries. As an economist, I have my choice of two very distinguished economists on the role of ideas. John Maynard Keynes's view was that, in the long run, ideas were much more influential than interests, and hence ideas could be autonomous from interests. And as an economist, I am also naturally sympathetic to arguments by that most famous of economists, Karl Marx. Perhaps his idea that in the long run has proved most influential—and most corrosive—is the argument that ideas themselves are a mere "superstructure" masking the true underlying economic interests of the powerful. This idea, with its literary and quasi-philosophical heirs in "deconstruction," has helped convince many in modern academia that conventional moral discourses are really attempts to construct social realities that justify (in part by masking) the exercise of domination. Interestingly, as we will see, many of the ideas that remain "undeconstructed" are those that justify restrictions on migration.

Here I examine both strains of argument. The next section begins with a more Keynesian approach to ideas and examines the notions that support the *moral legitimacy* of restrictions on labor mobility. A subsection below examines the self-interested arguments in the receiving countries (with the possibility, of course, that Marx and his noneconomist intellectual heirs are right and that economics is all that matters). In both sections, there are two interrelated questions. The first is why labor mobility is so unpopular in the citizenry at large. The second is why there are no strong advocacy groups attempting to change people's minds about their opposition. In particular, and of most concern to me as a development economist: Why are people who are concerned about global social justice and improving the lot of the world's poor not a pow-

---

5. Though it is very hard to be up to date on general opinions, it does not appear the attitudes toward immigration were getting better in the United States before the September 11, 2001, terrorist attacks, and this seems to have made matters worse. From 1992 to 1996, the fraction wanting immigration reduced rose from only 48.8 to 57.6 percent. In the aftermath of 9/11, there was an understandable backlash against "lax" control of the borders. In the aftermath, it was reported that almost two-thirds of Americans were in favor of halting *all entry of any kind* from countries suspected of harboring terrorists. But even the quite recent Gallup Poll in July 2003 reported that attitudes toward immigration in general are more negative than before 9/11.

erful advocacy group for greater labor mobility? These questions are related, because there is some possibility that if there were more effective advocacy, then perhaps ideas in the general population could be changed. But this will mean the discussion will veer a bit from "immovable ideas" persuasive to the general public (for example, the risk of terrorism) to ideas that appeal to narrower groups (for example, the impact on development).

"Moral" Arguments That Justify Restricting Borders

I want to begin with what might be phrased as the "moral support" for anti-mobility attitudes. I am not asserting that the ideas presented below are the *cause* of anti-labor-mobility beliefs, but I do make the conjecture that most people prefer to believe that their political and policy stances are not immoral, unfair, or unjust. In this section, I do not ask why people would prefer that people not cross national borders, but rather why people feel that it is *morally legitimate* to impose that preference. Why is it that people feel morally justified to use coercion to prevent people from crossing their national border to pursue voluntary economic transactions? And not only is that the prevalent attitude, but there is no truly significant agitation against that view from the development community. Addressing this question does not mean that the choices are "open borders" as a utopian "globally just" position versus the status quo; no policy issue is ever really decided exclusively on those grounds. The question is not the completely naive, disingenuous question of why "justice" is not the determinative consideration, but why these considerations have essentially *no* traction in current policy debates.

As an analogy, many people would prefer that the other people around them believe as they do in matters of religion (or, more broadly, culture). For millennia, when it was thought morally legitimate to use coercion to achieve that preference, the historical norms were forced conversions, forced suppression of alternative expressions of religious sentiment, and forced expulsions. In the modern world, although many people still have the same preference that others share their metaphysical views, it is no longer considered morally legitimate to use nation-state power and coercion to impose that preference. Why is it that the same broadening of views has no extended to allowing people born in other political jurisdictions to enter for economic reasons?

One possibility is that people in rich countries just do not care; they are completely morally indifferent to the fate of those outside their own borders. In general, this does not appear to be true, for one is able to generate substantial support in industrial countries for efforts to reduce global poverty through official aid, voluntary activities, and political activism. The total amount of official development assistance has hovered between $50 billion and

$60 billion and is again on the increase. This is not a particularly impressive total when measured as a fraction of rich-country income, but it does indicate some modest sense of moral concern. In fact, the fraction who report support for "economic aid to poorer countries" is more than three-quarters of the population in every industrial country (with the exception of the United States). In every industrial country (except Japan), a majority report that "too little" is being done to fight poverty in poor countries (table 3-5).

So the question is not why there is a complete lack of moral concern in rich countries; rather, the question is how this concern for global poverty is compatible with the view that it is morally legitimate to use coercion to prevent the entry of workers from poor countries into rich countries. Though global poverty does get attention, there is very near zero moral outrage or mobilization around the issue of increasing labor mobility. Four quick examples suffice. First, the 2005 "Live Eight" concert organized around the Group of Eight meeting at the Gleneagles resort in Scotland had a list—aid, debt cancellation, and improved trade—but no mention of labor moving at all. Second, the recent report of the Commission for Africa (2005), which is a serious and noble attempt to break the logjam on African development, proposed a large number of ideas for improving conditions in Africa—but it lacked an extended discussion of how allowing more labor from Africa is a positive step that rich countries could take. Third, the issue of subsidies to American cotton farmers received significant media and population attention in the context of the Doha round negotiations—explicitly from the "global justice" perspective of the impact on Chadian farmers. But the much more enormous distortion that farmers from Chad have to farm in Chad—and not farm in France, Poland, or Canada—was not mentioned. Fourth and finally, on a personal note, having recently spent four recent years (2000–4) on an East Coast college campus, I can attest that though there were protests against all manner of evils in the world—from conditions for laboratory animals to low wages for the university's own workers to conditions for workers *in their countries*—to my knowledge there was not a single rally against border controls. I never heard the chants "Hey ho, restrictions on labor mobility have to go" or "What do we

---

6. Another smaller example: I frequently fly on Lufthansa Airlines, which has a program of encouraging people to donate their spare change or small denominations of currencies they will no longer use to promote development activities as a way of addressing global injustice. In this context, an international flight in which *everyone being solicited is crossing a national border,* it is particularly noticeable that laudable moral concern for global injustice tends to be always channeled in some ways (charitable assistance from "us" to "them") and not others (letting people move across borders to work).

want? More access of the unskilled to rich-country labor markets! When do we want them? Now!" wafting across the campus.[6]

I believe four ideas underpin the notion of the moral legitimacy of restrictions. First, "nationality" is perceived as a legitimate basis for discrimination; second, there is strong "moral perfectionism"; third, there is a notion that development must be about nation-states, not nation*als;* and fourth, a set of ideas supports the notion that labor mobility is not necessary for prosperity. Two intertwined themes are addressed for each of these four ideas. The first is a positive assertion that these beliefs exist and underpin the legitimacy of attitudes toward limiting labor flows. The second theme is that (I believe) most of these ideas are, if not wrong, much less solid than the weight they bear demands.

Immovable Idea One: Nationality Is a Morally Legitimate Basis for Discrimination

There is a story that while perhaps apocryphal is nonetheless instructive. During its waning days, the international condemnation of South Africa's apartheid was intense in the United Sates. Protesters in the United States felt that it was morally intolerable that, in this day and age, a system would be maintained that sharply limited the mobility of people, that kept people in disadvantaged regions with no economic opportunities, that destined millions to lives without hope, and that split workers and their families—merely because of the conditions of their birth. A prominent antiapartheid activist was invited to come and give a series of lectures in the United States against the evils of apartheid in South Africa. But the trip was canceled because she could not get a visa to enter the United States.

It is said that fish do not know they are swimming in water.[7] The analogy between apartheid and restrictions on labor mobility is almost exact. People are not allowed to live and work where they please. Rather, some are only allowed to live in places where earning opportunities are scarce. Workers often have to travel long distances and often live far from their families to obtain work. The restrictions about who can work where are based on conditions of birth, not on any notion of individual effort or merit. The current international system of restrictions on labor mobility enforces gaps in living standards across people that are large or larger than any in apartheid South Africa. It is even true that labor restrictions in nearly every case explicitly work to disadvantage people of "color" against those of European descent.

The obvious response is that with apartheid people of the *same* nation-state were treated differently while the apartheid of international barriers to mobil-

---

7. Of course, they do not know much of anything else either.

ity is treating people of *different* nation-states differently. People subject to the same laws should be treated the same based on conditions of birth. The fact that people are, by whimsy of birth, allocated to different nation-states and hence treated differently has no moral traction. In nearly all modern theories of justice and ethical systems, most conditions of birth—one's sex, race, and ethnicity—are excluded as morally legitimate reasons for differences in well-being, and yet discrimination on the basis of nationality is allowed.

The case of sex is instructive. Tremendous attention is given to differences in schooling between boys and girls, in part because these are thought to be the result of morally illegitimate discrimination. Yet the differences in educational attainment between boys and girls *within* a poor country are often *an order of magnitude* smaller than those between boys in the poor country and girls in rich countries. For instance, in India, a country widely known for having a severe gender bias in schooling, the fraction of boys age fifteen to nineteen years in a survey in 1998–99 who reported completing at least grade nine was 44 percent, while among girls this fraction was only 33.5 percent—a shocking and, to many people, morally outrageous 10.5-percentage-point sex gap. But in nearly every OECD country, essentially 100 percent of girls complete at least grade nine—so the gap between rich-country girls and Indian boys is 56 percentage points.

Amartya Sen has popularized the notion of "missing women" in Asia due to differential death rates and (increasingly) sex-selective abortion. Because the child mortality rate in India is about 100 per 1,000 while it is 8 per 1,000 in the United States, this implies that 92 per 1,000 more Indian children than U.S. children die before age five. This means there are 2.2 *million* missing Indian children *each year*. However, while the "missing women" is a standard refrain, I have never heard the term "missing Indians" to describe the results of the child mortality differentials between the rich world and India.[8]

This is not to say that the problem of sex discrimination is not a serious global issue of unfairness. But what gives the sex comparisons such greater traction in the public mind—particularly in rich countries and in the development community—than the differences by nationality? Presumably, there is some sense that differences in well-being between the sexes within a country are "unfair" in a way that the massively larger measured differences in well-being across countries are fair. An Indian girl not having life chances equal to those of an Indian boy is widely regarded as morally unacceptable,

8. Almost as a perfect reductio ad absurdum, Nicolas Kristof in the *New York Times* has compared the low mortality rates in the United States to the even lower mortality rates in Singapore to discuss the issue of less than 20,000 missing Americans—with no mention of the issue that is smaller by orders of magnitude than the "missing" people in any poor country.

while preventing an Indian girl (or Pakistani, Bolivian, or Egyptian girl—or her parents) from moving across national borders to have the same life chances as a German boy (or U.S., French, or Japanese boy) is considered morally acceptable.

Carens (1987) makes a persuasive case that the natural extension of the currently "best" theory of liberal moral philosophy—Rawls's (1970) contractarian notion of social justice as condition that would be agreed to behind a veil of ignorance—would imply an ethical obligation for open borders.[9] In the Rawlsian view, sex discrimination is unjust or unfair because, not knowing if they would be born male or female, people would not agree to a social contract that produced a female disadvantage. But behind a "veil of ignorance," who would agree to a system in which some people are born in Niger (or choose any poor country) and some in Switzerland (or choose any OECD country) and those born in Switzerland are entitled to use coercion to prevent those born in Niger from enjoying life chances equal to those born in Switzerland? But the appeal of nationality as a legitimate category of discrimination is so powerful that philosophers are not sure whether this line of argument is a case for open borders or a reductio ad absurdum of the theory itself,[10] because any ethical theory that implied open borders was a moral necessity must be flawed.[11]

9. Interestingly, Nussbaum (2006) takes up the issue that the Rawlsian theory is not well suited to dealing with "nationality" as an issue. She proposes extending the "capabilities" approach to justice to the problem. In the end, her analysis ducks the issue of migration fully because her ten principles of a just world order provide generalities like "the main structures of the global economic order must be designed to be fair to the poor and developing countries" but then discuss minor issues in trade while ignoring the issue of labor mobility entirely.

10. In fact, Rawls himself argued that his "contractarian" constructions of justice applied only to existing nations. My understanding is that his quite coherent and plausible view is that no "natural extension" answers that question. This does not imply that border restrictions are morally just; it argues that the justice of border restrictions cannot be addressed.

11. There are other streams of thought about foundations for justice, such as "communitarian" positions that I do not discuss. In fact, I have a great deal of sympathy with a communitarian notion of justice that parallels Jürgen Habermas's approach to truth: A value moral system is whatever emerges from an continued, uncoerced dialogue about values within a community of practice. However, the one question such a notion of justice cannot address is the justice of physical exclusion from the "community." If the community is smaller than the nation-state, I would imagine that most nations would prevent communities from enforcing physical exclusion of others on "values" grounds—in fact, segregation was justified on precisely this "communitarian" grounds. If the "community" relevant for establishing a notion of justice coincides with the nation-state, this is a disaster. One can think of a long list of historical instances in which protecting the "community" and its beliefs led to physical exclusion (or expulsion)—but none of them positive. Though communitarian theories of justice are powerful and convincing on many grounds, I do not believe they can be relevant for this particular question.

The idea of "nations" that legitimates border restrictions is socially constructed or is an "imagined community" (Anderson 1991). That scholars have a hard time even defining what a nation is (Gellner 1983) makes the idea no less powerful. Nationalism and the distinct but related nation-statism retain a powerful hold on the international system—even *are* the system. Moreover, the idea of a nation has broad and wide popular appeal. People take it for granted that nationality is a morally legitimate criterion for differential treatment of people. But having a powerful hold on the popular imagination is not immutable—religion, race, sex, and ethnicity were considered legitimate grounds for discrimination for thousands of years.

Immovable Idea Two: Moral Perfectionism Based on "Proximity"

As seen in figure 3-1, there is a set of countries that have very high ratios of foreign-born workers to domestic population. The oil-rich Gulf States and Singapore have ratios of foreign-born to total population an *order of magnitude* higher than the similar ratios for many OECD countries. The UN *International Migration Report* explains that among the countries with the highest percentages of international migrant stock are the United Arab Emirates (73.8), Kuwait (57.9), Singapore (33.6), Oman (26.9), and Saudi Arabia (25.8).[12] These are compared in figure 3-1 with the ratios of the non-OECD-born population to total population in OECD countries (this eliminates, for instance, French or German populations in Switzerland or the United Kingdom–born population in Australia). Because our focus is on the mobility of unskilled labor, this better reflects the "labor absorption" of the economy. The highest-ranking OECD countries are Canada, Australia, and New Zealand, with about 10 percent of their populations born in non-OECD countries; the United States has 7.2 percent, the European average is 4.5 percent, and Japan has only 0.5 percent.

The countries with the highest ratios of foreign-born workers have created clear legal distinctions between "citizens" and "noncitizens," such that workers in these countries are explicitly not "migrants" with any expectation of achieving citizenship; nor do these workers have access to local labor markets but rather are licensed and regulated workers who are physically present to work. It is also the case that none of these countries is yet considered a fully functional democracy—and not only in the sense of denying these visiting workers political participation.

A common reaction to figure 3-1 is that these Gulf States are able to maintain these high foreign-born ratios because as nondemocracies they have less

---

12. Also among countries with high ratios of the foreign born are Jordan (39.6) and Israel (37.4).

regard for "human rights" than the OECD democracies. It is the case that these levels of distinctions between residents of the same country would be extraordinarily difficult to manage in more "democratic" countries. But this is not because democracies have more concern for a *generalized* notion of *human* rights that extends to all humans. After all, nearly all people who move to work in high-immigration countries do so willingly and nearly all those who stay do so willingly. There are long queues for admittance into these countries, even on the terms they dictate. By revealed preference, people are better off in Saudi Arabia, Kuwait, or Singapore than their alternatives.

What appears to distinguish countries that can tolerate very high levels of labor mobility from countries with low labor mobility is *not* that citizens of one or the other are *uniformly* more concerned about the well-being of noncitizens in the rest of the world. The difference is that the level of concern about the well-being of other citizens in countries with high labor mobility appears to be less connected with physical proximity than in the OECD democracies. That is, imagine a two-stage process in which, *first,* citizens of a country set the minimal well-being that will be tolerated among noncitizens living inside the borders of their country and then, *second,* these same citizens vote to decide the number of noncitizens to be allowed to enter their country. One can easily imagine that setting the first standard very high will lead to a low number allowed in during the second stage (because it is both more fiscally costly to society and a high cost to potential employers), while setting the standard low will lead to larger numbers.

It is perfectly plausible that setting a high standard for how people must be treated if they were to be allowed inside the borders makes people outside the borders much *worse off* because they are then not allowed in. Perhaps counter to one's intuition, if people in rich countries cared only about the *absolute* level of well-being of residents of poor countries—irrespective of where they were—these poor-country residents would be better off than if they care about them a great deal, but only when they are present in the rich country. Crudely put, most people in most industrial countries think that tolerating excessive differential treatment of people within their national boundaries is "immoral" but have few qualms about the suffering of people outside their boundaries—and think it acceptable to force people to stay outside. The level of deprivation of people in Haiti causes almost no direct concern in the United States. But if a Haitian manages to reach the United States, his or her very physical presence on U.S. territory creates an enormous set of obligations and political concern.

One of the intriguing features of the recent evolution of ideas is that it has become beyond the pale to think it is morally legitimate to discriminate against human beings because of the conditions of their birth—except for nationality. At the same time, concern for animals has been increasing. This leads to the obvious conclusion that close animals deserve greater moral consideration than distant human beings. Just as one example, in a recent review in the *New York Times Book Review,* Michael Ruse, a philosopher self-described as a left-leaning academic, lays out this argument quite clearly: "Personally I have a much closer relationship with my ferret than with the citizens of Outer Mongolia. Why should my actions benefit Outer Mongolians rather than my ferrets?"[13] He then goes on to say that perhaps his actions should benefit other human beings rather than his ferrets—but that an argument needs to be made. Imagine if the same author had used any other condition of birth. If a heterosexual white Anglo-Saxon Protestant were to pose the question "Why should my actions benefit a gay person or a woman or a Jew rather than my ferrets?"— even suggesting that such a claim needs defense would be unthinkable, scandalous. But curiously, being born in Outer Mongolia puts other human beings (who are physically distant) plausibly lower in the moral order of concern than a ferret that is nearby.[14]

Hence, an important idea supporting restrictions on labor mobility is the idea that while people are outside borders there is *no* ethical obligation at all, whereas if people are physically inside the borders they have to be treated (nearly) *equally.* Note that this is not a *universal* concern for human welfare— and in fact people from poor countries are plausibly *worse off* when the tolerated differences inside countries are *smaller.* Border controls are the use of coercion to prevent others from acquiring any of our moral concern or ethical obligation through physical proximity. Border controls keep the "Outer Mongolian" in "Outer Mongolia," in part just so that these distant human beings can be of less moral concern than close ferrets.

A common response to the idea that not all people allowed to enter a country to work would necessarily be entitled to all privileges of citizens is: "Who wants to live in the 'kind of country' where people are not treated equally?" But the fact is that we do live in a world of vast inequalities. The rich world is comfortable purchasing products from people who make very low wages— why not purchase services from the same people at the same wages? Even more telling, people from rich countries travel as tourists and receive services from people making very low wages. So there is no consistent objection of

13. This is in his review of *Human Nature* by James Trefil, July 4, 2004.

14. A recent book by the philosopher Martha Nussbaum treats three issues she believes create problems for the existing theories of justice: disability, nationality, and species membership. Again, how justice applies to non-nationals and how it applies to dogs or deer are treated as similarly important problems.

rich-country citizens to buying goods and services from people who make very low wages.[15] The objection is to doing so while the people are physically present in their country, which is extremely odd as a moral justification—particularly when the people would be present voluntarily. This is a truly selfish altruism because it uses restrictions to keep poor people out of one's geographic, and hence moral, vision.[16]

I conjecture that the twin ideas of the legitimacy of discrimination based on nationality and moral perfectionism based on proximity combine to produce in many people's minds the puzzling view that it is morally acceptable to use coercion to enforce an involuntary arrangement while a mutually voluntary arrangement would be morally unacceptable. That is, it is seen as perfectly morally legitimate as a nation to say "You may not enter my country to work and we will use physical coercion and its dangers to prevent you from doing so." This is not an idle threat—according to some sources, more Mexicans have died crossing the U.S. border in the past three years than convicts have been executed under the death penalty since its reintroduction in 1976. But somehow it is not seen as morally legitimate to make the offer: "You many enter this country, but on the following conditions that imply you voluntarily forgo, as part of the agreement to enter the country, certain benefits (but not all; basic rights are to be respected) to which citizens are entitled." The rejoinder to the "kind of country" objection is: "Who wants to live in the kind of country that uses coercion to perpetuate global inequality?"

I am conscious that this is standing the conventional wisdom for many who work on migration on its head. For instance, in a masterful survey of the theory and empirics of migration, Massey and others (1999) discuss the "Gulf system" of migration in unambiguously morally disapproving terms: "Nations of the Gulf thus sponsor strict labor migration regimes designed to maximize

15. The fact that only some people are willing to pay even a small premium for "fair trade" products is not a counterargument but only reveals how truly marginal this concern for low wages is.

16. There might be an argument that well-being is a relative concept, and hence that one is being altruistic by not allowing people to enter a country on unequal terms because they would feel bad if they were in a rich country because their self-assessed well-being would be lower because they are living near wealthier people. I personally have no patience with these types of "poor but happy" arguments. First, only voluntary arrangements that would allow, but not compel, mobility are discussed—the only nonpaternalistic way to decide how much the "relative" matters is to make the offer and let potential movers decide. Second, though certainly there is an important "relative" notion, it is to a "reference group" that may or may not be primarily determined by physical proximity—I conjecture Bangladeshis who work in the Gulf compare themselves to friends, relatives, and neighbors in their home country, not to emirs. Third, this same argument would suggest even stricter separation of people by economic status within a country.

the economic potential of the migrants as workers but to minimize their social participation as human beings" (p. 136). They argue that these "draconian" policies and shifts in nationality are designed so that "migrants can be more effectively exploited through policies of deliberate discrimination." But this view ignores the fact that moves to these labor markets on the explicit terms and conditions the countries set is an entirely voluntary choice of the migrants (with of course some exceptions), that millions of other Arabs and South Asians have benefited from access to these countries to provide labor on these terms, who otherwise would have faced even more difficult conditions, "exploitation" if you will, in their home-country labor markets. What could be more acknowledging of someone's status as a "human being" than to offer them a clear choice and allow them to make it? Perhaps unlike many other Americans, I have lived as an adult in Argentina, Indonesia, and India for two years each. In none of those countries could I vote, my presence was related to occupation, I did not have entitlements to social programs, the duration of my stay was strictly limited, and I had no path to citizenship. To say that I was therefore treated as less of a "human being" compared with the alternative of simply denying me entry into those countries is certainly not how I felt.

There is no question that this raises difficult issues that need to be discussed in a democracy. It is difficult to even put on the table for domestic policy consideration the fact that the apparently principled and "progressive" stance— "We will only allow people to work in our country who we also fully entitle with all the privileges of citizenship (or at least place on the path to such citizenship)"—can work to the massive *disadvantage* of poor people around the globe. The United States deals with this issue through massive cognitive dissonance and implicitly tolerating "undocumented" movers—who de facto do come on certain terms. Of course, open borders and "the welfare state" are incompatible with current global inequalities. But there is in fact a range of alternatives. It is very hard, however, to discuss how to balance the interests of maintaining a desirable society and polity as perceived by its current citizens with allowing labor mobility on some terms, mobility that would provide massive benefits to poor people from other countries.

Immovable Idea Three: "Development" Is Exclusively about Nation-States, Not Nationals

In his intriguing and important book *The Anti-Politics Machine*, Ferguson (1994) discusses the absolutely surreal descriptions of the economy of Lesotho in the reports produced by international development agencies. He points out that even though the people producing these reports were intelligent individuals and actually knew the reality of Lesotho, the constraints of the "development discourse" forced them into claims about the economy of Lesotho that were factually false, and ludicrously so. He argues that one of the necessary premises of the development discourse is that it must be about the economy of a *nation-state,* not the well-being of *nationals.* This primacy of the nation-state over nationals pervades the development discourse on migration.

This exclusive focus on "development" as the well-being of those who remain within a nation-state allows the reconciliation of the two views popular in the rich industrial countries: that "too little" is being done about poverty, but migration is off the agenda. One can only have the debate whether migration is good or bad for "development" if one construes "development" as synonymous with the well-being of the nationals who remain within the arbitrary borders of the political nation-state where they were born. But, as shown in chapter 1, if the gains to the *nationals* who move are counted as "development" to the country they moved from, then migration *is* development. Another way of putting this is that there is a "global poverty" agenda—improving the well-being of those below some globally accepted threshold (which need not be the penurious "dollar a day" standard; see Pritchett 2006). One could take the view that the "development" agenda was only that part of the global poverty agenda that dealt with improving people's well-being, provided they remained in a country classified as "developing." Though perhaps politically expedient, particularly when nation-states are the actors, this view does seem odd. There are two possible ways to reduce global poverty: migration; and increasing people's wages while in their home country. Why should only one of these ways count as "development"?

The exclusive focus on nation-states, not nationals, is revealed by the fact that while the growth rates of gross *domestic* product have been the subject of thousands and thousands of research papers, and gross national product at least nominally makes an effort to include the observed portion of income of nationals earned abroad, no one really knows much about the level or evolution of *nationals'* incomes or wealth. Take any of a number of small countries that have experienced substantial migrations, like El Salvador. Certainly the growth of the income of Salvadorans during the past thirty years must be massively higher than the growth of the per capita income of those Salvadorans who happen to live today within the borders of El Salvador.[17] Why should only

---

17. The same is almost certainly true of wealth, a subject that is rarely addressed. Even if only 10 percent of nationals are abroad, because their average wealth can easily be ten times that of those living domestically, the fraction of *wealth* owned by nonresident nationals can be a large fraction of the stock, which can play a key role politically (for example, the financing of social or domestic movements from bases abroad) and economically (for example, much "foreign" direct investment is of nationals).

the latter be counted as "development"? If "development" is about improvements in the well-being of people, then why exactly is location relevant?

A second example of the pervasiveness of the exclusive attention to the nation-state is the discussion of remittances as a "development" issue. There is currently a spate of literature taking the view that migration is good for "development" because it creates remittances. But remittances are only a central phenomenon if one sticks to the view that only what happens inside nation-state borders is important. Take two couples. One couple moves together to the United States, and the wife works; as for the other couple, the wife moves to the United States and the husband remains behind. Suppose in the two situations the total household income is exactly the same. With the separated couple, there are "remittances"—but the couple has to maintain separate households, and hence both actual costs are both higher (and there is the emotional cost of separation); so from a "development as well-being of nationals" view, the split migration is less preferred. But if one takes remittances as proving a connection with "development," then the split household is better for "development"—even though the people are worse off. Remittances are good almost entirely because they are good for the people earning higher incomes, part of which they remit, and do not need to be justified as a "development" of nation-state impact.[18]

The framing of "development" as exclusively about nation-states supports the notion that *preventing* mobility is morally acceptable because migration is itself bad for "development." In fact, there is even a popular movement to force rich countries to *not* recruit educated workers (such as nurses) from poor countries. Whether or not the movement of educated labor is good or bad for those in the country they move out of (and potentially back to) is a hotly debated question (Commander, Kangasneimi, and Winters 2003). But as a myth for supporting restrictions on migration, imagine the following, exactly symmetric argument: *Capital is good for development, therefore movements of capital out of poorer countries are bad for development, and therefore banks in rich countries should refuse to take deposits or investments from citizens of poor countries.* The day commercial banks refuse to take deposits from

---

18. The view of "remittances" as extra important because they provide a source of "development finance" also can, if unchecked, hark back to long-discredited "two-gap" models. That is, perhaps remittances are important because foreign exchange is itself a binding constraint on development, which would lead one to compare remittances (a portion of labor income of nationals that happens to cross nation-state borders) with sources of investment or foreign exchange, like official development assistance. There is currently no compelling evidence that remittances are "extra good" for economic growth.

citizens of poor countries, I will also believe that restricting labor mobility is supported by the idea that it is bad for development.

Immovable Idea Four: Labor Movements Are Not "Necessary" (or Desirable) to Raise Living Standards

People in the industrial world do care about the obvious huge and growing gaps in living standards between people in rich and poor countries. The quickest and most obvious way to increase the living standards of people is to allow them to move from where they are to a much richer country. One could be convinced that restrictions on labor movement were morally legitimate in spite of the obviously massive global inequities if one believed that movement across national boundaries was not really "necessary" to alleviate these inequalities. A series of ideas support this notion that labor mobility is unnecessary, but these ideas are either unproven or factually false.

First supporting idea: "Economic 'convergence' is a natural economic process," or "Capital mobility substitutes for labor mobility." The belief that the income levels of poor countries will "naturally" converge with those of richer countries that lack labor mobility makes it is easier to rationalize the legitimacy of barriers to labor mobility because differences are only temporary. That modern economic history *is* the history of absolute divergence does not seem to deter people from believing in absolute convergence.[19] The first generation of growth models—both Harrod-Domar and Solow-Swan—made capital accumulation the source of economic growth. The cross-national extensions of these models tended to assume that general productivity (often called "A," as a multiplicative factor that affects the productivity of all inputs) was equalized across countries by diffusion. In these models, if labor was abundant and A was diffused, then the marginal product of additional capital would be high (*very* high, as pointed out by King and Rebelo 1993), and hence capital would flow from capital-abundant to capital-scarce countries.

However, many researchers today are emphasizing that the main differences in levels of output per capita across countries are not due to capital (particularly as a causal factor; see Klenow and Rodriguez-Clare 1997) but rather

---

19. This has nothing to do with the recent debate in the economic literature about "conditional convergence," which was an important way of testing across two broad classes of economic models of growth. But "conditional" convergence is perfectly compatible with unconditional divergence if the "conditioning" variables are themselves diverging—which appears to be the case as both conditional convergence and absolute divergence are present in the data across countries.

are due to differences in the vaguely specified A—the general productivity term. As, for instance, Easterly (2004) has been pointing out, in "productivity world" (countries differ in A) many things are different than in "factor accumulation world" (countries differ in K). In productivity world, there is the possibility that both capital and labor would like to flow from poorer countries (with low A) to richer countries (with high A). Models in which A differs in large part due to differences in institutions—and hence capital mobility per se will not be equalizing—are attracting substantial empirical support (Acemoglu and others 2003; Rodrik, Subramanian, and Trebbi 2002; Easterly and Levine 2002, 2003). In an "all A" or "institutions rule" view of the determination of nation-state income, convergence is just one possibility.

Second supporting idea: "Trade is a substitute for labor mobility." In one very restrictive model of trade, under some empirical conditions, free trade in goods between two countries is sufficient for "factor price equalization." In this sense, trade in goods is a substitute for labor mobility because, with factor price equalization, there is no need for factors such as labor or capital to move. In this sense, trade in goods could be a substitute for movements of factors (including people), and hence reducing trade barriers to imports from country X could be seen as the substitute for allowing people to enter from country X.

However, the idea of factor price convergence as a rationalization of the typical stance that freer trade in goods is desirable but not freer mobility of people does not withstand scrutiny. First, as a theorem, the "factor price equalization" depends, among many other restrictive assumptions, on countries being sufficiently similar in factor endowments, which is an empirical condition that has no a priori reason to be true. Second, if trade were to cause factor price equalization, one would have expected to see more convergence of wages; but, as chapter 1 demonstrated at some length, wages have not been equalized. Third, in more complex models with multiple factors, trade can either be a substitute for or complement of labor mobility—so freer trade might promote *more* labor mobility. O'Rourke and Williamson (1999) present evidence suggesting that when markets for trade, capital, and labor were global in the late nineteenth and early twentieth centuries, freer trade was associated with *greater* flows of labor.

Third supporting idea: Aid is a substitute for migration. In contrast to increased migration, "foreign aid" appears to be quite popular. The third wave of the World Values Survey included questions on support for international foreign aid efforts. Foreign aid is enormously more popular than full labor mobility—for instance, 83 percent of Germans are in favor of aid, and 65 percent think "too little" is being done for poverty, but only 13.8 percent agree that Germany should "let anyone come"—and, as documented above, most would like migration reduced (table 3-5).

Fourth supporting idea: The world's poor are not so poor, or "it is all relative." One of the most pernicious myths is that the middle-class or richer people in poor countries are "really" not so poor. A particularly vicious ploy is to deflect all questions of *global* equity by focusing exclusively on inequality within countries. So there is always a great deal of attention given to the inequalities *within* poor countries. However, while there are of course some very few people from poor countries who are among the globe's millionaires and billionaires, these are the "super-rich" and are numerically unimportant. As illustrated in the recent *World Development Report* on equity and development (World Bank 2005b), the real, purchasing-power-adjusted "rich"—those in the 90th percentile of the distribution—are, in nearly every poor country, severalfold poorer than "the poor" (10th percentile) of OECD countries.

One response to comparisons of money income—even though they are adjusted for differences in prices across countries—is that they do not capture true "well-being." But any nonmoney indicator of well-being—child mortality, malnutrition, schooling—suggests that the richest fifth of the population in poor countries has a much lower living standard than the poorest fifth in rich countries. The child mortality rates of the *richest* quintile of households when ranked by an index based on the assets of many developing countries can be compared with the child mortality rates in OECD countries. Average child mortality in the OECD countries is about 6 per 1,000 live births. In most poor countries, the child mortality of the *richest* quintile is more than *ten times* that high. The idea that "the rich" of poor countries like India, Ethiopia, or even Indonesia are at anywhere near OECD standards of living by any measurable absolute indicator is just false.

A final response is that labor mobility is not really necessary for improving well-being because well-being is "all relative"—that, though the person in the 90th percentile in India is absolutely poorer than the person in the 10th percentile in the United States or Ireland, people only compare themselves with others around them, and hence "they" are perfectly satisfied where they are because if they came here they would be relatively worse off. There is certainly something to the argument that individuals assess their well-being by comparing themselves with others in a socially relevant reference group. But as an idea for supporting bans on voluntary labor mobility, it cannot work—let them decide.

Fifth supporting idea: Antiglobalization is the answer, not more globalization. A final idea that supports keeping labor mobility off the agenda is that the very limited and "everything but labor" globalization that has occurred is some-how the problem, and hence *less* globalization is the solution. It strikes me as remarkable that the well-justified moral concern of the youth in rich indus-trial countries for the world's poor is assuaged by *not* buying the products the world's poor produce (for example, the antisweatshop movement). But the same rich-country protesters who want better conditions in sweatshops, buy fair trade coffee, and protest U.S. subsidies to cotton (as a means of changing the World Trade Organization, or WTO, agreements) also do not question that the most benign future they can imagine is one in which the poor must continue to grow cotton in the Sahel (for slightly better world prices). These rich-country youth do not seem to ask why the poor are prevented by the coercion of their own democratic governments from taking the single action that would most assuredly raise their income. I was struck by the recent U.S. media coverage of the papal selection that in the brief biographies of several of the developing-world candidates it was highlighted, presumably as part of their appeal as papal candidates, that they were *opponents* of "globaliza-tion." That a quintessentially global institution like the Roman Catholic Church can think the "moral" position is "antiglobalization" seems beyond odd. The idea that *less* globalization is the answer prevents the obvious point—that true globalization includes labor—from even coming on the agenda.

Self-Interested Arguments against Migration

The ideas that restrictions on labor mobility are morally legitimate and not detrimental to the interests of the world's poor are perhaps a *consequence* of self-interested desires to limit labor mobility by the current citizens of rich countries than a *cause* of labor restrictions.[20] Almost certainly, the most immovable ideas that sustain restrictions on labor flows are those that labor flows do not serve the national interests of rich countries and that all else is, as they say, superstructure. My goal here is to not assess whether these ideas are true or false but rather to delineate the immovable ideas that must be at least shifted if increased flows of labor are to be permitted. That is, in the short to medium run, the design of policy proposals for increasing labor mobility must take these ideas as more or less given and then address the political constraints created by the ideas about the ways in which labor mobility is damaging to national interests.

---

20. On this issue of interests versus ideas, I find myself agreeing with Marx.

Immovable Idea Five: Increased Migration of Unskilled Labor Will
Worsen the Distribution of Income in the Receiving Countries and
Decrease Wages or Increase Unemployment

That an increased supply of unskilled labor would reduce the wages of unskilled labor is a straightforward application of supply and demand—and, as a statement about a "partial equilibrium" analysis, almost certainly true. There is of course an enormous ongoing debate about the *magnitude* of these effects; there is considerable evidence that they are much smaller than might have been imagined. An influential study of the influx of Cuban migrants into Miami from the Mariel boatlift found essentially no effects on either wages or unemployment (Card 1990). The resilience of local labor markets in absorbing new migrants was considerably higher than people thought. Nevertheless, though some might feel that scholars like Borjas (1999) overemphasize the negative distributive effects of the migration of unskilled labor,[21] the impact is real (not all immovable ideas are false).[22]

This is not a review of the economic literature on the effects of migration on unskilled wages but about the impact of this *idea* on opposition to increased labor flows. There is reasonable empirical evidence that people's attitudes toward immigration are compatible with the view that they see immigration as worsening the conditions for unskilled labor. For instance, opinion surveys reveal that less skilled workers are more likely to oppose both freer trade and increased immigration (Scheve and Slaughter 2001; O'Rourke and Sinnott 2003; National Research Council 1997). This joint opposition to trade and labor movements is important, because economists have typically seen opposition to freer trade as an obstacle to overcome through the design of liberalization efforts (for example, the Multi-Fibre Arrangement as a political device to overcome opposition caused by the potential loss of textile jobs in the United States, "safeguard" policies, and so on) rather than as an argument against freer trade.

Timmer and Williamson (1998) make an important argument that the rising inequality caused by immigration combined with the extension of the

---

21. For example, my perception is that his book tends to emphasize the impact on the "less than high school" native workers, a category for which the estimated effects on wages are large but which are a small fraction of the labor force, rather than the "high school educated," for which the impact is quite modest.

22. The National Research Council (1997), in a review of the literature on the demographic and economic effects of immigration, concluded: "The weight of the empirical evidence suggests that the impact of immigration on the wages of competing native-born workers is small—possibly reducing them by only 1 or 2 percent."

franchise led immigration policy to become more restrictive in the late nineteenth and early twentieth centuries. Using evidence from a number of host countries, they conclude that the timing of the onset of restrictions on mobility is well explained by these changes—without any appeal to any other force, such as "anti-immigrant" attitudes.

In many ways, this notion that migration "takes jobs" is an "immovable idea" because of the typical person's "intuitive economics." The education specialist Howard Gardner (1991) talks of the difference between how the "intuitive" and "expert" approach similar topics. For instance, every person has a working theory of how physical objects behave—an intuitive physics— which is usually correct over a large range of common phenomena (for example, rocks will drop, chairs will stay in the same place, elastic bands will snap back) but makes *systematic* mistakes when pushed into unfamiliar territory.[23] Many people approach trade policy with a mistaken "intuitive economics": that exports are good and imports are bad is based on an intuitive economics that mistakenly extrapolates what is true of the firm—sales are good (profit increasing), while purchases are bad (profit decreasing) for the nation. Most people think about labor markets in terms of numbers of jobs as a discrete phenomenon (perhaps because they extrapolate from personal experience; they either have a job or do not), and hence political debates tend to get framed in terms of numbers of jobs, whereas all economic models posit wages as clearing a labor market and the number of jobs and wages as jointly endogenous. Many people's views on labor mobility depend on whether or not they perceive that migrants "take jobs away" from existing workers (whether natives or previous migrants).

This is about the political traction of the idea that because it lowers the unskilled wage and increases wage inequality, labor mobility should be opposed. Though the general popularity of the notion might not have much to do with economists, it is worth a word or two about the economists' response to this idea. The economists' typical response to objections to potential Pareto-improving policies that worsen the income distribution is to say "Instruments to targets." That is, nearly any macroeconomic or microeconomic policy reform—trade liberalization, airline deregulation, macroeconomic stabilization—will produce some change in the economywide

---

23. His memorable example is asking people about the trajectory of a ball shot out of a barrel that is shaped like a corkscrew. A majority of people untrained in physics think it will continue a corkscrew trajectory—which is a mistaken application of the principle "things will continue to do what they were doing."

income distribution. But the usual approach is to recommend a policy if it is *potentially* Pareto improving and to also recommend that broad distributional concerns be addressed through the best available instruments for redistribution. That is, there is a broad tradition (to which many object but is nevertheless widespread) that one cannot burden every single policy with a complete general equilibrium analysis of not only the aggregate but also the distributional impact of each policy and use every policy as a distributional instrument. Rather, the "instruments to targets" literature suggests that the most effective policy is to have the best instrument for each target. In this view, while any policy (say trucking deregulation) might have distributional consequences, the policy recommendation should maximize output with one set of instruments and redistribute with another.

Rodrik (2002) emphasizes that imports from countries with low wages that embody an equivalent (relative) amount of unskilled labor should have exactly the same impact on wages if they affect the net supply/demand balance for unskilled labor in exactly the same way. But when applied to trade, nearly all economists will agree that this is a "second best" problem. This is not a reason that justifies tariff restrictions as an instrument to improve income distribution. That is, in this instance, most economists have argued that policies should be separated and that income should first be maximized (free trade) and then optimal transfers implemented.

Hence, it is not clear why this same argument does not apply to the actual mobility of labor (abstracting for a moment from the potential fiscal costs of migrants). I am relatively certain that none of the economists who use evidence of the distributional consequences of increased flows of unskilled labor as an argument against increased labor mobility would be comfortable with that exact same argument as a reason for banning imports from these same places. There is an argument that the "instruments to targets" approach is inadequate in general because although governments could use other, more effective instruments to address distributional implications, they *will not* in fact do this. But again, this is an equally valid reason to oppose imports of labor-intensive goods (which economists almost never do) as it is to oppose migration (which economists often do).[24]

---

24. Whether economists should do this is in fact a complex question. Some now advocate a complete distributional analysis of each policy and adoption of only those that are desirable (perhaps by some "do no harm to the poor" or appropriately inequality-weighted welfare metric standard). This is not yet the typical economist's view.

The main point is not about economics or economists, but that labor mobility is unpopular because in the mind of the general public, and in the minds of many less skilled workers in rich countries, it is perceived as a cause of lower wages for those whose wages are already low. Any proposal for labor mobility must tackle this issue head on, and we will return to it in chapter 4. The fact that this issue has been dealt with for goods trade but not for migration suggests that there are also other issues with labor mobility—so onward.

Immovable Idea Six: Movers Are a Fiscal Cost Because They Use More in Public Services Than They Pay in Taxes

One popular idea is that migrants are a net fiscal cost—they consume more in publicly provided services than they pay in taxes. There are huge debates about whether this is empirically true or not. A U.S. National Research Council study concluded, at current configurations of taxes and the benefits and structure of immigration, "the annual fiscal impact per U.S. resident of an increase of 100,000 per year in the immigrant flow under the baseline circumstances . . . to be roughly +30 $/person, composed of +40 $/person at the federal level and −10$ per person at the state and local level" (National Research Council 1997). But more important, as to whether any given estimate is better or worse, there is no correct answer to the question about the net fiscal cost, for two reasons.

First, even within a given structure of mobility, "the" fiscal cost has no single correct answer because it is entirely contingent on the structure of immigration—by age, by education, by family composition. Younger migrant workers with no children pay far more in taxes than they receive in benefits. Migrants with low education and earnings who bring children constitute a net fiscal cost—because of publicly provided education. Notice that the studies in the United States show the net fiscal impact varies from positive for federal government and negative for states because of the differences in the taxes collected and services provided at the various levels. This emphasizes that there is no way to extrapolate these results from the United States to any other country, because they would differ in the structure of taxation (direct versus indirect taxes) and benefits.

Part of this is the idea, commonly repeated, that "open borders" and the "welfare state" are incompatible, which is true. But this has nothing to do with labor mobility, unless one *presumes* that every person who is physically present in a country necessarily acquires a set of claims on benefits. That is not true. The laws about the distribution of benefits can be structured in nearly any way countries choose (subject to fundamental rights or constitutional constraints).

A country may choose to have a minimum entitlement payment (independent of whether the person works or not) as part of its social benefits (and there is no compelling reason not to have such a benefit). In wealthy countries, this minimum may be far more than people in poor countries earn by working. It would be impossible to have "open borders" and a scheme of social protection that makes these benefits available to everyone who is physically present. But this does not mean that a "welfare state" and "increased labor mobility" are incompatible. No one imagines that the welfare state and massively increased tourism are incompatible—because physical presence as a tourist creates no claims on social benefits.

More to the point, it is widely accepted for skilled labor that a "temporary physical presence" to provide services does not imply claims on social benefits. Management consultants, business executives, academics, and financial professionals travel the globe and are admitted into countries to provide specific services. Moreover, the expansion of this particular aspect of labor mobility is pushed very hard by rich countries. But no one objects that these people do not acquire citizenship or entitlements to publicly provided services in the countries where they work.

This is an extremely sensitive issue, but it must be tackled. The argument that it would be "unfair" or "immoral" to have social benefits for one set of people physically present in a country (say, citizens) and not make those same (or similar) benefits available to another set of people (say, temporary workers) is, to my mind, based on a deeply flawed notion of fairness. For example, one person is living in Chad and another in France (or any other two countries), and France could offer that person two distinct packages of benefits: (1) allow the person to be physically present in France to provide a service on a continuing basis (with no implication of access to France's "labor market" more generally); or (2) allow the person to participate in the scheme of social benefits to which all French citizens are legally entitled. The notion is that because French voters are unwilling to offer the citizen of Chad all the benefits of package 2, then it is "unfair" to offer them on a voluntary basis the benefits of package 1 at a lower fiscal cost to voters. I cannot think of any rationale for this as a moral argument. I cannot see how either of two major strains of reasoning, Rawlsian "contractarian" or Nozick's (1974) "process fairness," can be made to justify such a position—that if they cannot be offered packages 1 and 2, it is unfair to offer them (on a voluntary basis) just package 1. After all, the person from Chad can always refuse package 1 and be no worse off.

This leads to the second main point about fiscal cost: One cannot simply assume that the incremental fiscal cost of an additional worker in a new

scheme of labor mobility would be the same as the cost per person under current existing immigration flows. The new migrants might enter under entirely
different conditions—or themselves be different in important ways.

The point is political. People *believe* migrants create a fiscal cost and for
this reason oppose additional migration. But this fiscal impact depends on the
configuration of migration and the structure of benefits provided to migrants
(and their children). Proposals must address the issue of fiscal cost if they are
to be politically viable.

Immovable Idea Seven: Allowing Movement across Borders Creates Risks of Crime and Terrorism

The terrible and tragic events of September 11, 2001, obviously changed the
entire discourse about immigration policies in the United States. Similar inci-
dents in other countries, such as the train bombing in Spain and the killing of
a prominent filmmaker in the Netherlands (apparently for his "anti-Islamic"
films), have created similar concerns that an excessively liberal policy toward
allowing non-nationals into the country raises security risks. There is no question that a country must secure its borders against those that present a threat,
and any serious proposal for labor mobility across borders must take this concern very seriously.

The issue of the relationship of crime and labor mobility is distinct, with
two dimensions. First, there is a perception that migrants are more prone to
criminal activity. Most research suggests, not surprisingly given that migrants
are self-selected, that migrants are much *less* likely to be engaged in crime than
are the native born (National Research Council 1997; Butcher and Piehl
1998). But it will always be the case that some crimes are sometimes committed by foreigners; and, unlike crimes by the native born, these crimes will be
perceived as "avoidable" in ways that similar crimes committed by citizens are
not. The risk of criminality must be addressed.

Second, there is the issue of the vicious circle, in which, by definition, many
immigrants are committing a crime. Many countries, in particular the United
States, have resolved their social and political ambivalence (and open political conflicts among various interests) about labor mobility by creating laws
that then are not enforced. Though increased migration is opposed in opinion polls, there is also a sense among many that these laws are illegitimate and
hence that there is little reluctance to employ people who are not present in
the country legally. The fact that many candidates for high political appoint-
ment have violated the law by employing individuals who are undocumented
migrants suggests deep ambivalence about the legitimacy of these laws. The
problem with resolving the pressures that people do want to hire foreign

workers, even if undocumented, with the desire to control the borders with an expensive political charade at enforcement is that crime and migration *are* intimately associated.

Again, the analogy with Prohibition is instructive, for the attempt to ban the consumption of alcohol meant that people who consumed alcohol were breaking the law and even those who opposed Prohibition were left with an uneasy sense that law and order should not be flaunted. So, the upshot is that if labor mobility across borders is a crime, then laborers who cross borders are criminals. The whole of what is otherwise a perfectly ordinary process— no one talks of workers being "smuggled" from Michigan to Arizona— acquires a taint of illegitimacy. So both drugs and people are "smuggled" across borders—but there is a qualitative difference, because drugs are illegal on both sides of the border, but people working for other people is the most ordinary thing in the world on both sides of the border. The solution, far from easy—as the United States has learned—is to create an enforceable regime of labor mobility.

Immovable Idea Eight: "They" Are Not Like "Us"— Culture Clash Arguments

Of all the ideas that limit migration, perhaps the most important is the idea that there is a national "culture" and that increased labor mobility threatens that culture. This is also the most difficult to discuss in a sensible way, because it is so difficult to separate this argument from garden variety racism, bigotry, and intolerance. That is, if anyone were to suggest that a person who is already a citizen of an industrial democracy ought to be treated differently because they were Jewish, or Muslim, or Hindu, the person making that suggestion would have clearly moved beyond the pale of intellectual and political dis-course and would be treated as a complete crank. But if someone were to sug-gest that people should not be allowed to enter that same country because they are Muslim and that this would change the "character" or "culture" of the country, then these people would, and do, constitute a serious political force. In a tour de force demonstration of the pliability of political logic, one pro-minent European politician argued that Muslims could not be allowed in because *they* (the Muslims) were intolerant—and hence, in the interests of toleration, people with different beliefs could not be tolerated.

The point is not to argue against this idea or even to argue that these ideas need to be changed. The point is that there is a deep-seated distrust of people from countries that are "different" and that this is a powerful political force that needs to be addressed in any proposal for greater labor mobility.

Summary

One way of summarizing the self-interested arguments against labor flows is to think of the basic economists' classification "goods" according to whether they are rival and/or excludable—leading to their classification as private (excludable and rival), public (nonexcludable, nonrival), club (excludable but nonrival), and commons (rival but nonexcludable).[25] Access to a country is clearly an "excludable" good; the question is the benefits of exclusion. If the benefits of being in France are primarily "rival"—an additional person's presence in France reduces the benefits to those already in France—then this is a "commons" problem, and a lack of excludability would lead to a "tragedy of the commons," in which the value of being in France was eroded by allowing more people into France. Conversely, if the benefits to France are access to France's "institutions" that allow for law and order and high economic productivity (as in the "all *A*" or "institutions rule" theories of national income discussed above), then, as long as there are no congestion effects, this is a public good and there is no reason to exclude, and hence "physical access" is a club good.

A key question is whether the factors that make rich countries attractive as migration destinations are "rival" goods or not. The answer is that they are a mix of pure public goods (like high-quality institutions for economic productivity), club goods (for example, access to public schools), and "common" goods (for example, law and order). The ideas that oppose labor mobility tend to emphasize the "commons" aspects (for example, foreigners dilute our culture, or foreigners do not pay their way fiscally)—where additional people reduce the value—while downplaying the "public good" aspects.

Why Try and Put Labor Mobility on the Development Agenda?

Labor mobility has been completely off the "globalization" and development agendas, for two reasons. First, these agendas are constructed by and for *nation-states*, and, as we saw in chapter 1, whatever secondary benefits migration might have for the nonmover citizens of immigrant-sending or -receiving countries, the main beneficiaries are those who move (and their families). Second, the ideas blocking increased labor mobility in the rich industrial countries seem so *immovable* that it was simply not worth wasting time and energy pushing against them. Personally, as a development economist, I had always avoided working on issues of labor mobility because while freer trade

25. I would like to thank Michael Woolcock, a sociologist, for this suggestion.

in goods or more capital mobility or even economic aid had obviously viable political constituencies and coalitions, it seemed pointless to even talk about the mobility of unskilled labor because the political obstacles were insurmountable. But as I thought more about it, four arguments convinced me that increased labor mobility is an issue worth raising.

First, ideas are less immovable than they seem. Ideas are a bit like a large dam. A dam can hold against tremendous pressures for decades and even centuries; but once breached, it can disappear in hours. In 1914 nearly every European state was headed by a monarch, a form of government that had persisted in Europe for more than a thousand years; but twenty years later, a blink in historical time, all but a few of the European monarchies were gone. Even more telling, the very *idea* of a monarchy as even a *possible* mode of governing was gone. Colonialism persisted for centuries—and then essentially disappeared in the two decades from 1947 to 1965—and the very *idea* of colonialism disappeared with it. Slavery had been a part of a multitude of civilizations for thousands of years—and was rarely considered morally problematic—and it too disappeared in the blink of the historical eye.[26]

The ideas that supported monarchy, colonialism, and slavery seemed in their day solid, impregnable, and respectable. Not only did these ideas change, but they changed so decisively that, even a few decades later, people wonder how otherwise rational and well-meaning people could have been held in the thrall of such patently ludicrous, not to mention obviously morally despicable, notions. Abolitionists in the United States were a small, radical, and many thought lunatic fringe group almost right up to the time they completely changed history forever; and it is now almost impossible to believe that they were the fringe.[27]

It is not inevitable, or perhaps even plausible, but it is at least *possible* that the idea that it is acceptable to place restrictions on the movement of persons that hold human beings cruelly hostage to the place of their birth will be seen by my grandchildren as hopelessly wrongheaded. What seems like prudence and realism today in not promoting what seems "politically impossible" may seem a simple lack of moral courage tomorrow.

Second, as I read the pages of publications that consider themselves socially and morally "progressive," my impression is that there are at least ten times as

---

26. There are many other examples of persistence followed by rapid change from the trivial—ranging, for instance, from the disappearance of dress hats for men to socially beneficial attitudes about highway litter.

27. John Brown was executed for treason and then celebrated as a hero within years.

many books about a political movement with a moral stance that is broadly characterized as "animal rights" than there are promoting increased unskilled labor mobility. Though these arguments might not yet cut much ice in the real world, serious, thoughtful people are suggesting that our descendants will look back at us in disbelief with the moral callousness with which we ignored the rights of animals in the same way we regard the casual racism of our ancestors. They suggest that those of us who stand on the sidelines today in the struggle for animal rights risk being seen with hindsight as just as morally feckless as those who tolerated slavery or segregation. To me, this concern for animal rights seems like the reductio ad absurdum of the view that all that matters to morality is physical proximity. There are human beings on the planet who do not live as well as do animals under the minimal, *legally enforced,* standards for animals in the United States.[28] These people are trapped in their present and future condition of poverty by, among other forces, the coercion exerted by citizens of rich countries to keep them out of their country. I cannot predict what the future will bring, but I hope that it will judge me more sharply for the extent to which I worried about the plight of my fellow human beings, even people of different colors and in the distant parts of the planet, than my pets at home. If there can be a justice-based movement for animal rights, certainly there can be a justice-based movement for labor mobility.

Third, the antiglobalization movement gives me great hope—although I believe it is almost entirely wrongheaded. The movement gives great hope because it generates political impetus around actions to improve the well-being of the poor. The fact that one can create "fair trade" action groups and protests about unfair cotton subsidies and concerts for debt relief suggests that there is not complete indifference. But the problem is not that globalization has gone too far. Perhaps "everything but labor globalization" has gone too far, but globalization has not even begun to face the key issue for the poor: the market for unskilled labor (Cohen 2005).[29] Instead of attempting to

28. For animals used in laboratory research, there are published guides on the quantity and quality of food, living conditions (space, light, temperature control), and access to health care (both preventive and curative).

29. This is obviously a play on Rodrik's influential book *Has Globalization Gone Too Far?* (1997) versus his colleague Robert Lawrence's *Has Globalization Gone Far Enough?* (2004). But Rodrik's "Feasible Globalizations" (2002) begins to put labor on the agenda and to make the point that it has, so far, been an "everything but labor" globalization, which is not the only possibility, because expansions in labor mobility are "feasible" and have a high payoff.

roll back globalization, it seems that there is scope to generate progressive social movements to push globalization ahead.

The final element that convinced me to think about migration was reading a Harvard Business School case extolling the success of a very few people in the pharmaceutical industry using domestic politics and an existing international process for negotiation—the General Agreement on Tariffs and Trade (GATT) / WTO rounds—to create more favorable conditions for their industry. GATT had always been about removing barriers to trade and lowering tariffs. To my knowledge, no economist had ever considered the fact that different countries adopted different types of patent legislation as a "trade" barrier—after all, patents create property rights, and countries differ legally in a myriad of ways about what is, or is not, "property." But the pharmaceutical industry placed it squarely on the negotiation agenda for a WTO round. How is it that patent protection is so strongly on the WTO agenda but labor mobility—an issue of near infinitely more importance for human well-being and much more naturally a "trade" issue—is not? If blatantly self-interested advocacy can so easily sway what is and is not on the international agenda, then perhaps the prospects for a serious agenda on labor movements is not impossible.

Conclusion

A set of interrelated ideas sustains the political coalitions and popularity of rich-country policies to restrict human movements, a system that resembles apartheid on a global scale. Though I have presented the eight ideas that make these seem morally acceptable, it is possible that these are really rationalizations driven by opposition to labor movements that is in turn driven by narrowly self-interested concerns. Let me list the ideas here in reverse order:

8. "Culture clash"—"they" are not like "us"—foreigners are, well, foreign.
7. Security—crime and terrorism—foreigners are a risk.
6. Fiscal costs—movers do not pay their fair share of taxes.
5. Inequality—allowing entrants to the labor market makes the poor already here worse off.
4. Labor mobility is not necessary to improve the plight of the world's worst off.
3. Development is about nation-states, not nationals.
2. Physical proximity is all that matters for moral obligation.
1. "Nationality" is a legitimate basis for discrimination.

Because the main forces blocking increased labor mobility are ideas, and I hope I have captured the most important of these ideas, the challenge is to develop alternative ideas—proposals for national and international agendas that create development-friendly policies toward migration and create sustained pressure for the adoption of those proposals. The next chapter addresses the various aspects of proposals that are both *politically acceptable* to voters in rich countries and also *development friendly*.

4

Accommodating Forces and Ideas to Achieve Development-Friendly Labor Mobility

Deep economic forces are creating increasingly irresistible forces for the movement of people across national boundaries in response to economic opportunities. The rich industrial countries' existing policies toward migration and labor mobility attempt to resist that tide. These policies limit the flow of laborers across borders and distort the composition of the flow. Worse, because these policies are inadequate to address the economic pressures, which come from employers on one side of a border and potential workers on the other, the excess pressures are currently relieved by pushing people into extralegal channels that create negative effects for the movers, limit the potential development impact, create an aura of illegitimacy, and further taint the notion of labor mobility in the rich countries.

The existing policies are the result of ideas held by the citizens of the rich industrial countries (about both what is morally legitimate and what is in their self-interest). There are two ways to create political circumstances more favorable to increased development-friendly labor mobility: either change ideas or create policy proposals crafted to accommodate those ideas (at least in the short to medium run). Though efforts to change ideas are important, in the short to medium run, politicians and policymakers cannot be expected to flout their own constituents' views. Even politicians who lead from the front are not pioneers. Can politically acceptable mechanisms for labor mobility be devised that accommodate the immovable ideas, while still remaining development friendly?

In this chapter, I review three policy options that are currently under discussion. As would be expected in an effort to reconcile the irresistible and the immovable, each of the three has positives and negatives:

—One policy direction that has proven politically acceptable is to increasingly propose making *migration* decisions based on personal characteristics, such as skill, wealth, and nationality. These proposals buy increased political acceptability, but at some expense in their development friendliness.

—A second policy direction is to bring labor mobility onto the international agenda via the World Trade Organization (WTO). My view is that this mechanism, though potentially development friendly, will have a difficult time being made politically acceptable at any significant scale.

—A third policy direction, which has gotten perhaps the least attention (until quite recently), includes proposals for mechanisms to increase the temporary mobility of unskilled labor in politically acceptable ways, framed explicitly as a development agenda. The bulk of this chapter is devoted to outlining the characteristics of desirable proposals of this type.

The next three sections analyze the three types through the same lens—how well they accommodate the eight immovable ideas of chapter 3, while remaining development friendly, with some ideas for how to mold these proposals.

Before moving to the discussions of these three types of proposals, I want to highlight several caveats about the discussion of policies and their political acceptability. First, this is not meant as an exclusive list of the options, and an important point is that in this domain one needs creativity and innovation. In particular, I would not want anyone disappointed with the options discussed below to conclude that because this set, or my discussion, is inadequate that therefore there are no viable options. Second, none of these have to be mutually exclusive. Countries could have more of each, or some countries more of one (WTO) and other more of another (bilateral deals). Third, this discussion is deliberately short on details, because it is more focused on getting the foundations for classes of proposals down than on working out or advocating any one of them, which is the next step.

High-Skill-Based Policies Are Winning Rich-Country Debates about Migration

The main policy proposals on the agenda are increasing attempts to create a more attractive and favorable regime for highly skilled (or just plain wealthy) migrants. In their recent book *Give Us Your Best and Brightest*, Kapur and McHale (2005) document the general move in policies aimed at attracting the highly skilled. In its review of its member states' migration policies, the Organization for Economic Cooperation and Development (OECD) documents at least some moves toward more "high-skill-friendly" migration policies in nearly all countries. As part of the Copenhagen Consensus process, Martin (2004) reviewed the opportunities to address global challenges in migration. He argued that the greater use of skills in selecting permanent migrants was an, and perhaps the only, attractive opportunity for addressing the challenge of migration.

There are many examples of attempts to attract highly skilled workers for specific industries. The United States has always had a mechanism for allowing persons of "extraordinary ability" to obtain citizenship (which many argue has been key to the rise of American universities to their global position). In the United States, there are also mechanisms like the H-1B scheme, which allocates a certain number of visas a year for "specialty occupations," which for example were used in the Silicon Valley to help build the computer industry. Even Germany, which is not famous for having been migrant friendly, has recently initiated legislation to attract the highly skilled for their graduate training and for employment and as a means to maintain and build biotechnology industries, because it fears losing its historic advantage in these fields. The National Health Service in the United Kingdom has been recruiting medical personnel from countries that were former colonies.[1]

On a broader scale than industry-specific actions, Canada and Australia have migration policies that allocate access to the path to citizenship by "points." For instance, in the Canadian scheme, there are a total of 100 possible points from each of 6 factors (for example, including education, experience, arranged employment, and languages). In the education category, a potential immigrant can get up to 25 points (for a Ph.D., for instance). The Australian system also provides points for various skill and work experience categories (for instance, various skilled occupations with shortages receiving relatively more points). There are many who argue that the United States should adopt a more skill-friendly migration policy. Borjas (1999), for instance, has been a powerful academic advocate of the view that if one evaluates *immigration* policy (about who might take up permanent residence or citizenship) strictly from the view of the welfare of the *existing* citizens of the *recipient* coun-

---

1. In an interesting twist, the police in the United Kingdom have been under pressure to increase minority representation in their ranks (presumably with a view to making them "more like" the communities they police), and recently the police suggested meeting the targets for minority representation by hiring abroad.

try, then (1) the welfare gains are small from additional migration and (2) the distributional effects of allowing unskilled (relative to the host-country labor market) migration are negative (in that it lowers the relative wage of the most disadvantaged).[2] His proposal therefore is to (1) reduce (or cap at its current levels) the total amount of immigration and (2) change the formula by which migrants are chosen to place more weight on items like education and potential economic contribution and less on "family reunification."

Meeting the "Eight Ideas"

Table 4-1 is an organizing device that I will use throughout this chapter to summarize the analysis of how existing classes of proposals for increased migration meet the five forces and the eight ideas. Proposals for making migration policy more skill friendly are perceived as politically feasible because they address the immovable ideas of rich-country citizens. However, the way these proposals meet the political constraints in rich countries perhaps limits their development friendliness. Rather than listing the ideas in the order of chapter 3 (and table 4-1), I start from the strong points and work toward to weak.

The strongest argument for more highly skilled migration is that it has a more equalizing distributional impact and will not lower the wages of unskilled workers in the immigrant-receiving country more than equivalent numbers under the existing schemes. Arguably, one of the largest problems rich societies face is that the apparently skill-biased economic progress of the past few decades has increased the demand for skilled labor faster than the supply and hence lowered the unskilled wage relative to the skilled (and in the United States lowered the unskilled real wage in absolute terms for an extended period).[3] This skill bias is the largest part of the reason behind the enormous increase in the skill premium in more flexible labor markets like the United States and combined, with the more rigid labor markets in Europe, a rise in unemployment there. It is difficult to mobilize labor unions or mass politics

---

2. Because this is a key issue concerning the mobility of unskilled labor, it is hotly contested, with views ranging from large negative effects to next to zero to—if one adds certain features to general equilibrium models—even mildly positive. Whether or not the evidence he presents for the empirical magnitudes of these effects is compelling is, to some extent, beside the point, because the point is that politically the issue must be addressed given that many people believe it is true.

3. Acemoglu and others (2003) discuss the evidence for a "skilled-biased" change in technology as an explanation for the recent evolution of labor markets. More general assessments of the cause of the rise in the skill premiums in the United States are in Katz and Murphy 1992. Davis (1992) addresses the issue of the similarities and differences with Europe.

Table 4-1. *Analysis of Proposals for Increasing Migrant Quality*

Proposal	Increased emphasis on high skill / wealth	Summary
Five forces for increased labor mobility		
High and rising wage gaps	−	Equalizes wages only at the upper end (if at all)
Differing demographic destinies	+	Limited impact if allows more migration
Everything but labor globalization	−	Detracts from globalization of unskilled labor
Employment growth in hard-core nontradable services	+/−	Does not necessarily focus on "hard-core" nontradables
Ghost/zombie countries	−	"Brain drain" effects possibly large (for example, health care workers from Africa)
Eight ideas limiting migration in industrial countries		
Nationality is a morally legitimate basis for discrimination	+++	Points systems can be nationality adjusted
Moral perfectionism based on "proximity"	++	Those who are allowed are expected to become citizens
"Development" is exclusively about nation-states, not nationals.	− −	Detracts from "development" to the extent it exacerbates "brain drain"
Labor movements are not "necessary" (or desirable) to raise living standards	− −	Does not help with labor
Increased migration of unskilled labor will lower wages and worsen the distribution of income in the receiving countries	+++	Does address inequality problems in receiving countries
Movers are a fiscal cost as they use more services than they pay in taxes	+++	By attracting higher wage migrants reduce fiscal cost
Allowing movement across borders creates risks of crime and terrorism	+++	Points systems allow careful screening of applicants
"They" are not like "us"— culture clash	+++	Language and education screening can be used to increase "compatibility"

against allowing a few more computer programmers, doctors or (somewhat less so) nurses, biochemists, or economics professors.[4] Moreover, these concerns about policies that might further widen economic and social inequalities are very real, and their importance should not be minimized.

An important aspect of many skill-based schemes is that they have specific numerical quotas to be used in particular (or a range of) occupations, for which it is declared that there are insufficient recipient-country nationals to meet the "need." This aspect is important because it meets the intuitive economics of citizens (see chapter 3), who think in numbers of jobs rather than wages or wage differentials.

A second strong argument for high-skill migration is that it allays fears of migration causing net fiscal costs. Obviously, if wages increase with skill and taxes are, in general, more progressive than expenditures, then admitting migrants with higher skills lowers the net fiscal cost. Almost certainly, admitting very highly skilled migrants has net fiscal gains.

Three additional attractive aspects of programs for selective admission of the highly skilled are that they preserve the notion of nationality as a legitimate basis for discrimination, reduce the fears of "culture clash," and reduce fears of crime and terrorism. Rightly or wrongly, my conjecture is that the typical rich-country citizen feels less threatened by admitting doctors, engineers, and academics from any specific country than by allowing in the unskilled from the same country. Similarly, people feel (almost certainly correctly) that the highly skilled and wealthy are less likely to be engaged in crimes that people most worry about (such as violent street crime) than are the less educated or wealthy. Finally, one need not assume that the more highly educated are less likely to be terrorists, but security checks in such programs for migration or mobility of the skilled are thought to be enforceable because the highly skilled are more likely to have a traceable paper trail (for example, diplomas, résumés, passports, and travel history), whereas the unskilled are almost invisible to a formal system of background checks.

Allowing and even recruiting highly skilled labor scores well on the "self-interested" ideas that block labor mobility—but less well on the "moral" ideas. In particular, if one is concerned about the less well off in the world, then this idea has two primary defects. First, concerns about "brain drain"—of which there are several—imply that those concerned about "development" are gen-

---

4. As an aside, American academic economists are safe from charges of hypocrisy in arguing for more labor mobility because the top end of the market for economics professors is completely open to international competition, particularly at the very top. In the top five American economics Ph.D. programs, a substantial fraction of the faculty is foreign born.

erally not in favor of selectively recruiting the most highly skilled. Particularly when it comes to health professionals, this has generated a substantial backlash because of concerns for the erosion of health system capability in poor countries.

Second, a very strong point in favor of allowing high-skill migration is that it *reduces* income inequality in rich countries (primarily by lowering the wage premium on skills). But, by exactly the same logic, the departure of skilled labor should increase the skill premium in the immigrant-sending countries.[5] This is a concern, because within-country expenditure inequality is already *much* higher in most developing countries than in most developed countries (World Bank 2005b). Moreover, while the economist's response to concerns about policies that increase inequality in rich countries may plausibly be "instruments to targets" (as it is generally with these issues in trade; see chapter 3), nearly all poor countries lack adequate low-cost tax and effective redistribution instruments. Increasing inequality is an even larger problem for poor countries than rich ones because there are fewer viable policy "instruments" to address the problem.[6] So even if the economic effects are symmetric (unskilled mobility would increase inequality in rich countries; skilled migration would increase inequality in poor countries), the social effects could be asymmetric because inequality is more easily mitigated in rich countries— while the inequality created in poor countries by rich-country migration policies would be more difficult to cope with.

My sense is that *immigration* policies in rich countries (which is one subset of broader policies affecting labor mobility) will move increasingly toward using skills (and wealth) in the migration decision.[7] The strict, if slightly heartless, logic of maximizing the economic gain to only existing residents of the recipient countries suggests migration policies that "recruit" the best of the rest. My prediction is that the brain drain problem (if it is a problem) will only get more severe as more and more countries tailor their immigration policies

5. This may or may not increase inequality, because if the more educated leave, the distribution of skills among those remaining is more equal, so then even if the skill premiums increase, measured inequality could go either way.

6. Two major themes of the economic historian Peter Lindert's (2005) work are that (1) the historical evolution of the now-rich countries led to greater and greater tax effort (ratios of tax to gross domestic product), in part because with economic modernization it became easier to collect at low direct and indirect cost, and that (2) most of this revenue was devoted to "social" spending, which was inequality reducing.

7. For instance, the United Kingdom has recently (June 2005) announced proposed changes in migration policy that emphasize skills—and reduce or eliminate temporary unskilled labor, except from EU countries. Home Secretary Charles Clarke was quoted thus: "The route to settlement is through skilled labour" (BBC, June 21, 2005).

to attract migrants of higher potential economic contribution. The question is, what stance should the governments of poor countries (and those who care about the fairness of the global system) take toward those policies?

One stance is to oppose rich-country immigration or labor mobility policies that actively recruit skilled persons. I would be cautious about attacking policies that recruit the highly skilled for three reasons. First, as reviewed above, the evidence is not so clear that the "drain" dominates the "gain" when the highly skilled are able to move to rich countries. When countries have fundamentally sound economic policies, the exposure to other countries, industries, and practices may well bring positive benefits—even when a large fraction stays permanently—and when policies are unsound, more human capital alone is unlikely to make much difference (see Pritchett 2001, 2004b).

Second, even if it were the case that the net impact of the mobility of a highly skilled person on those remaining in the sending country was negative, restrictions on the mobility of the highly skilled in poor countries is a highly inequitable tax to pay for the global public good of poverty reduction.[8] Third, I have never seen the argument for why human and physical capital should not be treated symmetrically. One could argue that if a people were forced to increase their investment in the domestic economy even if they got higher returns elsewhere, this would have an important "external" effect by raising the overall capital stock. Yet "capital flight" is a pervasive phenomenon, and, as Collier, Hoeffler, and Pattillo (2004) have documented, a huge fraction of wealth held by Africans is held outside Africa—one suspects that in most large countries, a much larger fraction of financial than human wealth is put to work abroad. As far as I know, no industrial country has objected, in principle, to receiving investments from residents of poor countries (except of course for concerns about corruption, laundered money, and so on). Preventing individuals from moving their human capital to higher returns, while allowing (or even encouraging) them to invest their physical wealth abroad, seems to create perverse incentives and signals.

---

8. Think of it this way. Suppose the wage in the sending country is w_s, the wage in the recipient country is w_r, and the total economic cost to the sending country of losing a highly skilled person is C_s (per capita is C_s/N). Suppose $w_r - w_s > C_s$, so that people would be willing to pay an "exit tax" that left the sending country no worse off. This is essentially funding the costs by imposing a tax on those who could move, even though they are much poorer than, say, the typical person in the receiving country. Now, of course, if the highly skilled persons have received public-sector subsidy of their education with the presumption it would be domestically used (and hence taxed), then paying the full cost of that subsidy if they work abroad does seem equitable.

The other response is to mitigate the potential negative consequences of "skill-based" policies in rich countries. First, one way in which the brain drain is less important than might be thought is that the possibility of migration draws people into schooling or training by raising the returns to schooling, even if only a few migrate successfully.[9] So, for example, though there are many nurses in the United States from the Philippines, it has been argued that this has expanded the total number of nurses trained in the Philippines and that the actual domestic supply has increased, not decreased (though this has yet to be tested definitively). The incentive effects of increasing the returns to education through the possibility of migration are potentially large (as one example, the expansion in "English medium" schools in the private sector in India since the beginning of the economic boom has been very rapid). One complement of high-skill policies is to match recruitment with support to the supply side in the sending countries, so that the *net* domestic supply is not reduced. So perhaps, rather than a ban on recruiting nurses from African countries, a combination of increased support for the training of nurses plus recruitment would actually benefit both countries.

A second means of expanding the "development friendliness" of skill-based policies that are occupationally based, such as the H-1B visa as opposed to those that are general means of filling a total for migration as in Canada, is to accept the general movement toward numeric quotas for specific skilled occupations, but also to push to broaden the category of skilled occupations. For instance, if countries allow nurses, then this category can perhaps be expanded to "home health care workers"—which are required to have some special-purpose training and to work in that specific occupation but for which the skills are more easily acquired abroad.

The third means is to link proposals for unskilled *labor mobility*—for either variety discussed below—to the trend in immigration policy toward a higher "quality" of migrants. The fundamental difference between "labor mobility" and "immigration" policy is that *immigration* implies a relatively permanent movement, while more neutral (if ungainly) terms like "temporary movement of natural persons" or "labor mobility" convey less a sense of right to perma-

---

9. The obvious analogy is with professional athletics in the United States, where a few athletes making astronomical salaries induce a much broader supply response, so the net number of baseball-playing Dominicans is probably increased, not decreased, by the recruitment of Dominicans into professional baseball in the United States. In fact, a study by Milanovic (2003) of soccer (football) shows that the increased commercialization and competition among football clubs has increased the quality of national teams in poorer countries as they capture the increased skills of their nationals leaving for the higher-quality (and better-paying) leagues in Europe—a gain from "leg drain."

nent residence or citizenship or even generalized access to the labor market. The trend for immigration policy to be more skilled biased in rich countries is likely inexorable; there can be attempts by sending countries and the global community to create linkages with labor mobility—a package deal. So, for every biochemist, computer programmer, or doctor who is admitted, the same country will also expand access for an unskilled worker—even if only temporarily and on limited terms.

Can the WTO Move Beyond "Everything but Labor" Globalization?

The first section discussed the ways in which countries are addressing migration unilaterally, in which policies are moving toward more active recruitment of highly skilled persons or investors. A second way in which labor mobility is coming onto the global policy agenda is through the mechanism of the WTO. Within the General Agreement on Trade in Services (GATS), there is a framework for negotiating the "temporary movement of natural persons" (TMNP) in connection with the provision of services, which is called "mode 4" because it is the fourth mode of the provision of services (see table 4-2). In principle, foreign companies could negotiate access to a domestic market for services—such as cleaning hotels and office buildings or landscaping homes or offices—and then negotiate the ability to place workers in order to carry out these contracted services, even though these workers themselves do not have access to the host-country labor market. An obvious agenda for research and policy advocacy is to help developing countries with a labor surplus to develop proposals for the significant expansion of labor mobility under the GATS mode 4 as part of the Doha (or following) round of WTO negotiations. Winters and others (2002) discuss many of the aspects of temporary labor mobility under GATS, particularly the possibilities for expanding TMNP.

The WTO (and its predecessor, the General Agreement on Tariffs and Trade, or GATT) has made important contributions to the world economy by creating a powerful mechanism to harness domestic and international pressures for reducing barriers to trade. However, the very same principles of the WTO that make it a powerful institutional mechanism for liberalizing trade in goods also make it difficult to create politically viable agreements on labor. The WTO is a framework for negotiating and enforcing agreements among countries about their economic relationships, but what has made it powerful is that it is a framework with basic *principles*. Three general principles are embodied in the articles of GATT and the rounds of negotiations: *most favored nation* (MFN), *prices not quantities*, and *reciprocity*. These principles will not apply to

Table 4-2. *Summary of Analysis of GATS Mode 4*[a]

Proposal	GATS mode 4 within WTO	Summary (assuming MFN)
Five forces for increased labor mobility		
High and rising wage gaps	+	Would allow movement in unskilled services
Differing demographic destinies		Could be used to fill gaps
Everything but labor globalization	+++	Brings labor mobility into the globalization framework
Employment growth in hard-core nontradable services	+++	Focuses on services trade, including those services that require physical presence to deliver
Ghost/zombie countries		No special emphasis
Eight ideas limiting migration in industrial countries		
Nationality is a morally legitimate basis for discrimination	− − −	MFN would extend "market access" to all countries
Moral perfectionism based on "proximity"		
"Development" is exclusively about nation-states, not nationals	+++	Nation-states negotiate agreements via WTO
Labor movements are not "necessary" (or desirable) to raise living standards	−	
Increased migration of unskilled labor will lower wages and worsen the distribution of income in the receiving countries	− − −	Allows opening of markets in unskilled labor
Movers are a fiscal cost as they use more services than they pay in taxes	+/−	Since presence would be temporary not a major concern
Allowing movement across borders creates risks of crime and terrorism	− − − −	"Market access" and MFN is very difficult to reconcile with security concerns
"They" are not like "us"— culture clash	− − −	MFN implies countries cannot control nationality of service providers

a. GATS = General Agreement on Trade in Services; WTO = World Trade Organization; MFN = Most favored nation negotiations on labor mobility because they run head-on into many of the immovable ideas.

A basic principle of the WTO negotiations is MFN, whereby any agreement reducing trade barriers between any two parties is automatically extended to all other signatories[10]—so that if the United States agrees with France to reduce tariffs on French cheese and in return the French reduce tariffs on U.S. wheat, these tariff reductions are extended to cheeses of all nationalities by the United States and all countries' wheat by the French. Every country that is a partner in the overall negotiation is treated as well by each other country for each good as the MFN is treated. This principle creates a powerful downward dynamic of restrictions by automatically extending bilateral agreements multilaterally. However, extending the bedrock principle of MFN to agreements on labor mobility runs head-on into three of the immovable ideas.

First, the principle of MFN directly contradicts the idea that a person's nationality is a legitimate moral and political ground for differential treatment. MFN applies only awkwardly to the movement of persons, because (whatever the ideals of universalism) people have nationalities in a way that goods do not. National origin can be treated as an incidental feature of a ton of steel in a way that people feel national origin is not an incidental feature of persons. Though the equal treatment of equivalent goods irrespective of national origin is perceived as "fair," the same is not true of persons. Every country's laws make distinctions about persons based on national origin, and MFN has never been a principle in immigration laws.

Second, people feel very differently about people from other countries for reasons of cultural heritage, ethnicity, language, and historical background. The idea of "culture clash" is incompatible with applying MFN to agreements about labor mobility. So, for instance, one can imagine Germany making a bilateral agreement with eastern European countries (even those not currently within the European Union) to allow their construction firms to bid for construction services in the German market with the agreement that they can provide their own workers to carry out the construction (and hence TMNP). But it is difficult to imagine Germany (or any other OECD country) entering into a binding international agreement whereby whatever access it provides to its market for construction services to one country (perhaps one with some historical or cultural ties) is *automatically* extended to all other countries.

---

10. The fact that regional agreements have not respected MFN is precisely what has made them so controversial (even when people agree they are "trade-creating" reductions on barriers).

Third, and perhaps in the current world most important, security concerns are going to be overwhelming. One could imagine a GATS mode 4 negotiation in which countries link supplies of, say, "motel cleaning services" to the ability of rich countries, say the United States, to place its executives abroad (or provide financial consulting services or any number of skilled occupations for which the United States wants a physical presence). This might mean that the foreign-based *employer* chooses the persons who then have access to the territory of the United States to provide the services. The United States is going to have different treatment of the persons, depending on their national origin, so access will not be "MFN" to TMNP in that sense in any case. The security objection that will be raised to giving "market access" to a foreign firm on an MFN basis is insurmountable. Imagine the announcement that an Iranian firm had won the service contract to clean every Motel 6 (now a French-owned chain) in the United States, and hence 50,000 persons of this Iranian firm's choosing would be branching out to every major city of the United States. A similar analogy could be created for nearly any OECD country with at least some poor country.

Because MFN so clearly contravenes the immovable ideas, while it creates a downward dynamic on barriers to trade, it may create an *upward* dynamic on barriers to TMNP. An agreement that might be reached bilaterally about the movement of X Mexicans to the United States, Y Vietnamese to Japan, or Z Moroccans to France would not be reached if, because of MFN, this were extended automatically to X, Y, and Z persons of unspecified nationality.

A second basic principle of the WTO is "prices not quantities"—that is, trade barriers should be in the form of tariffs and not quotas (or other nontariff barriers).[11] This is a hard principle to apply to services trade of any kind, where the barriers are usually issues like regulation, certification, and so on, and hence barriers are often more subtle. But I cannot imagine moving to an environment of labor mobility with "tariffs," because every country reserves the right to determine the *numbers* of persons crossing its borders; in particular, this would create enormous concern about the equalization of unskilled wages and hence distributional concerns. In fact GATS is very specific in stating that even mode 4 negotiations are not about giving individuals access to a country's labor market. That is, the idea of TMNP is not labor market access that a specific service is contracted for and the person enters a country with the purpose of

---

11. Again, this principle has had important exceptions (or varying legal status in GATT): the Multi-Fiber Arrangement, agriculture, "voluntary" export restraints, agricultural restrictions in the form of quotas, and so on. But these were always recognized as violations of the "spirit" of GATT.

providing that service. This already implies that the agreements are more about quantities, not prices, and imply administrative control of the process.

A third basic principle of the WTO is reciprocity—that the negotiations involve one country "giving up" access to its national market in one product in order to "gain" market access in another product. As much as economists dislike this entire line of rhetoric, this notion of reciprocity has been an important element of the domestic political economy of multilateral trade agreements. The genius of reciprocity is that it pits exporting interests against import-competing interests in the same country, so that when legislators are considering the treaties and are lobbied by industries that will "lose jobs" if import barriers are lowered, they can also be lobbied by exporters who will "gain jobs" from access to export markets. If the issues can be "delinked" (that is, a country can gain export access without import liberalization), this weakens domestic support to general agreements.

Reciprocity will be difficult to establish for labor mobility in unskilled labor because the linkages are distant. WTO negotiations are broken into areas; for instance, in the Doha round negotiations, there are negotiating areas such as agriculture, services, nonagricultural market access, intellectual property, and dispute settlement. Linkages are easiest within areas (trading off one type of agricultural protection), and agreements across areas are more complex (reducing agricultural barriers in return for changes in dispute settlement). It is not at all clear what labor surplus developing countries will "give up" that powerful interests in the labor-importing countries want.

My argument is that there are difficulties in using the GATS mode 4 as a framework for negotiating, "scheduling," and enforcing agreements of labor mobility for the provision of services. If the traditional WTO principles of MFN, prices not quantities, and reciprocity do apply, then agreements are unlikely to be politically feasible in the OECD countries. But if these traditional principles do not apply, it is not clear why the WTO is an attractive framework for negotiating these agreements. That is, if individual OECD and other host countries are to negotiate bilateral agreements with sending countries about specific numbers of persons allowed for specific services that are not part of a reciprocal trade arrangement, it is not clear why they would want to bring this under the umbrella of the WTO.

I believe these arguments are consistent with the experience of GATS mode 4 to date. Very little of the global trade in services flows through mode 4. The WTO estimates of services trade in 2000 state that 28 percent was "cross border supply" (mode 1), 14 percent was "consumption abroad" (mode 2), 56 percent was "commercial presence," and only about 1 percent was "temporary movement of natural persons" (mode 4). Very few agreements have been scheduled under GATS mode 4, and it is not currently a major element of the ongoing Doha round negotiations.

One could argue that although GATS mode 4 agreements would raise political opposition, the WTO in general and the Doha round in particular have enough momentum to "carry" labor mobility agreements, and hence this would be an opportunity to link a weak agenda (labor mobility) with a strong one. My view is perhaps the opposite.[12] The WTO process is currently weak, with little broad-based political support in many OECD countries, and the prospects for a successful conclusion of the current round of negotiations are only fair to middling—even without the inclusion of a significant element on the mobility of unskilled labor. In fact, one of the strongest rhetorical points for developing countries to use in trade negotiations is that reportedly used by then-president Carlos Salinas de Gortari of Mexico in discussions of the North American Free Trade Agreement: "Take our goods or take our people." In other words, if the OECD countries want to avoid pressures for immigration flows, making the national economies grow fast is possibly the most effective instrument. However, though this might be a good way to get a better deal out of the Doha round for developing countries, this is not going to lead to useful labor mobility agreements.[13]

My rather pessimistic conclusions about the use of the GATS mode 4 are a positive prediction, a conjecture, not a normative statement. The GATS mode 4 is an existing mechanism in a multilateral agreement and should be pushed to be as successful as it can possibly be. That is, nothing here should be taken as critical of GATS mode 4 agreements if they can be reached. My conclusion is that, if one is interested in promoting greater mobility of unskilled labor, I would not rely exclusively or even primarily on GATS mode 4 as the instrument. That said, GATS mode 4 is an existing international instrument, and its

12. This chapter was first drafted in 2003—before the events in Mexico, in which negotiations were broken off early, and Hong Kong (in 2005). As readers peruse this, they will know more about how "strong" the impetus for the conclusion of a "development round" was—but so far (May 2006) my argument that the Doha round can barely carry itself has good odds.

13. As somewhat of an aside, in spite of the above arguments, I believe the labor surplus countries should prepare proposals for unskilled labor mobility as part of GATS mode 4 as a way of strengthening their hand in the overall WTO negotiations. I am convinced by those who argue that the developing countries gave up more then they have gotten in the most recently concluded round (for instance, on Trade-Related Intellectual Property Services), in part because interests in rich countries had specific proposals on the table and they pushed them politically. In the overall negotiations, there cannot be concessions in the abstract—only if there are specific, WTO-compliant proposals for the mobility of unskilled labor officially on the negotiating agenda can these be "given up" in the pursuit of other interests (for example, the reduction of agriculture subsidies) as part of the negotiation.

limits have not really been explored, in part because there have been few well-articulated proposals for large-scale unskilled labor mobility. Until this is pushed ahead, it is impossible to know its limits. One action of the global actors could be to assist poor countries in developing proposals.

Six Accommodations: Features of Politically Acceptable, Development-Friendly Schemes for the Temporary Mobility of Unskilled Labor

A third way to reconcile the forces and pressures for increased mobility with the political opposition and still maintain policies that are development-friendly policy proposals is with six *accommodations*. I use the term "accommodations" to emphasize that no economist working from first principles would ever arrive at these particular features.[14] These features are not desirable objectives, but they are compromises that make other desirable objectives perhaps politically feasible. The six accommodations that agreements should incorporate are

1. be *bilateral* agreements between host and sending countries,
2. allow for *temporary* movement of persons in a regime *separate* from immigration,
3. have numerical *quotas* for specific occupational categories (and internal regions in the host country?),
4. enhance the *development* impact of the labor movement through agreements with the sending-country government and voluntary arrangements,
5. enlist sending-country enforcement by imposing automatic penalties on the sending country (and host-country employer) for laborers who overstay, and
6. protect the fundamental human rights of laborers.

The trade-offs among labor migration schemes discussed so far are pretty stark. The proposals that are politically popular generally move in the direction of being even less beneficial for the world's poor than the current incoherent policies (in which family reunification and asylum/refugee status play

---

14. Working from first principles of economics (and perhaps moral philosophy, for that matter), one would likely arrive at proposals for the full integration of markets for goods, capital, *and* labor, even across politically distinct sovereigns, as happened within federal countries like the United States historically and is happening within the members of the EU today. But abstract first principles and politics rarely mix, and this is no exception. In an analogy with physics, when forces meet resistance, this creates friction and heat, and workable systems need to accommodate these side effects through lubrication and cooling.

a large role). The proposals that almost certainly would augment unskilled labor demand—such as using GATS mode 4 as a mechanism for market access for "natural persons" to supply nontradable services (for example, cleaning, gardening, waiters), perhaps as employees of foreign-based subcontractors— are politically unpalatable and hence are currently, more or less, off the table. The question is whether there is something in between these two extremes that would make explicit concessions to rich-country politics to accommodate the immovable ideas about migration while still creating some role for a greater movement of unskilled labor from low-wage to high-wage countries.

Accommodation One: Bilateral Agreements (Perhaps under an International Rubric)—or Perhaps Regional Agreements

The first feature is that all agreements would be *bilateral*—or more accurately *unilateral*—decisions of the receiving country with the agreement of the sending country to participate. In the end, domestic politics will dictate that each country have control over who may or may not enter its borders, and that this will not be part of any general international or multilateral *binding* commitment.[15] The obvious exceptions are true integrating unions like the European Union that may choose to adopt a common policy. Pushing for multilateral agreements along the lines of the WTO is unlikely to be successful.

This is not to say that international organizations would play no role. Figures like Jagdish Bhagwati (a prominent academic and former senior adviser at the WTO) openly advocate the completion of the organizations that facilitate the global system by creating a World Migration Organization. Existing international organizations are increasingly, albeit tentatively, bringing migration onto the policy agenda. The United Nations established a Commission on Migration, the International Labor Organization is increasingly involved, and the World Bank has recently published several major reports and studies (World Bank 2005a, 2005b) and has even established an internal working group on migration. The International Organization for Migration (IOM) has existed since 1951 (it was originally founded to assist with the repatriation of displaced Europeans) and has recently taken a more active analytic and advocacy role— for instance, with its new flagship publication *World Migration 2005*.

Any international organization is likely to play a "light" rather than "heavy" role because there is no incentive for any attractive rich-country destination to cede any degree of sovereignty over its migration policy—and important incentives not to. An organization may play some role in encour-

---

15. This is particularly true of policy in the United States, which historically has been very leery of any binding international treaty or commitment.

aging agreements—particularly agreements that are development friendly or facilitate learning from experience through research and advocacy. It is even conceivable that countries would allow a review of their migration policies along the lines of the International Monetary Fund's article 4 consultations or the WTO reviews of trade policy. These "light" roles are not unimportant, particularly if one believes that in the long run ideas are what matter.

Accommodation Two: Temporary Admission, Not "Migration"

The second accommodation is that access to the labor market be temporary. There are always multiple windows for legal presence in a country. One of those windows would be access with the ability to work (which is constrained; see below), where that access is explicitly temporary. There are two issues with temporary programs: feasibility and desirability.

The conventional wisdom is that "temporary migration is permanent and permanent migration is temporary." It is thought to be politically or administratively impossible to enforce "temporary" schemes, while at the same time many individuals who initially move "permanently" return to their home countries. This conventional wisdom grew out of the experience with the Turkish "guest workers" brought into Germany in the 1960s. But as a general proposition, it is belied both by countries with very large temporary worker populations (such as Singapore and Saudi Arabia) and by successful long-term occupation or activity-specific programs, such as those for agricultural or seasonal labor (for example, the tourist industry) in many countries or occupation-specific programs like the au pair J-1 visa in the United States. The conventional wisdom is right: Temporary labor mobility must be appropriately structured to ensure compliance. But it is not right that large-scale temporary programs are "impossible"—even in democracies—yet they do require other accommodations (described below).

The second question is whether the "temporary" is desirable as a politically motivated accommodation that would politically allow larger flows (and stocks) of unskilled foreign-born labor or whether the very fact that admission was "temporary" would create negative reactions. For instance, Mark Rosenzweig (2004) has argued that much of the political opposition to migration comes from "culture clash" arguments that perceive unassimilated foreigners as a social (if not actual physical) threat and that by making the stay of new arrivals in the host country explicitly time limited this discourages assimilation: "It is doubtful that creating a large *permanent* population of temporary, unincorporated immigrants, who would have no incentive to learn the host-country language or adopt its cultural practices, would engender support for immigration. Indeed it is likely the opposite" (Rosenzweig 2004, p. 16). I will return to this argument in the next section as I argue that the political economy of temporary migrants depends on how they are employed.

One additional benefit to schemes for temporary mobility over permanent migration is that, at least potentially, it increases the number of people who benefit. One objection to labor mobility, especially as a "development" agenda, is that, even with the best possible political schemes, the number of movers will always be very small relative to the developing-country population—and hence this is a "lottery" approach to poverty reduction. In comparing increased admissions of workers with more standard development projects, the benefits are much more certain and much larger *per person* for allowing workers to work for five to ten times their current wages merely by moving than for any known development intervention. But, for instance, estimates of the aggregate benefits given in chapter 1 (and below) are based on the *stock* of developing-country migrants being higher by 14 million people, out of a developing-country labor force of 2.5 billion—so 1 in every 200 people. This means that the benefits of allowing more workers are like a lottery—large gains to very few people. But the gains per person and the total number of people who benefit from a change in the stock of migrants depend on the flow. If the rich country's political economy tolerance is based on the *stock* of foreign-born workers, then programs that allow many workers a short (one- to five-year) chance to work will benefit many more people than migration with a longer duration. For instance, suppose the host-country tolerance is 1 percent of the sending country's stock and that as each cohort enters the labor force it is allowed to work abroad. If the average duration were shortened from fifteen to three years, the fraction of workers who would have some work abroad would increase from 3 to 15 percent of the sending country's stock.

Accommodation Three: Specific Occupational (and Regional) Quotas

The third accommodation is that the permission to be in the country would be based on *specific quotas* in *specific occupations* (and perhaps even regions).

Before talking further about quotas, I want to propose a revisionist interpretation of the Multi-Fiber Arrangement (MFA) under GATT. I know this is risky because, for most economists who work on international trade, the MFA is a *bad* example because it was developed in open defiance of the important GATT principles—(1) it had bilateral quotas; (2) it imposed quotas rather than tariffs; and (3) it was essentially nonreciprocal, in that the countries it was imposed on never "agreed" to the restrictions but instead allowed their exporting behavior to be regulated by the arrangement.

However, my revisionist interpretation of the MFA is that U.S. producers were so uncompetitive in textiles that a sudden exposure to imports would cause rapid changes in employment, and because textile industries were concentrated, this would lead to local and regional economic disasters. Therefore the idea of the MFA was to ease the transition of the decline of the textile industry—that is, it was not conceived as a "safeguard" for unfair trade nor as a "breathing space" measure for a fundamentally sound industry that would be viable in the long run to get back on its feet but simply to smooth the personal and local disruption of the decline of a regionally concentrated industry. And it attempted to do this without blocking the rise of exporters by not imposing quotas on a specific item from a country until it reached a threshold and by allowing the quotas to rise every year.

The key question is whether it would have been politically possible to achieve the GATT round agreements without the MFA. If not having an acceptable side arrangement on textiles would have in fact scuttled GATT, then MFA looks enormously successful because (1) the rounds did happen; (2) exporters of textiles were not stymied—South Korea, Taiwan, Hong Kong, and others all managed to sustain enormously rapid increases in textile exports in spite of the MFA, so one cannot argue that it was an insurmountable obstacle to success; (3) it did in fact smooth declines in employment in textiles because, for instance, U.S. employment in textiles has fallen dramatically; and (4) eventually it is going away, so it was a (very long) transitional measure.

Something like the same logic is at play with unskilled labor mobility: Without controls, there are dangers that migration will cause local disruptions to the labor market and place the already disadvantaged at further disadvantage. For instance, a huge concern for social policy in the United States is that the real wage for unskilled labor has fallen—because it creates all kinds of social problems as the lack of "good jobs" in urban areas leads to low labor market attachment (and the attractiveness of informal and criminal activities) and social disruption because family formation and stability are at risk (Wilson 1996). Even though my view is that the evidence is weak that the increased levels of migration in the United States are a significant factor in these trends in the labor market (skill-biased technical change, per Acemoglu and others 2003, and other factors are the major culprits),[16] even the risk of exacerbating these social problems is unattractive.

---

16. The evidence of the Mariel boatlift of a huge influx of workers into a single labor market (Miami) shows little impact on employment or wages (Card 1990). Even Borjas's (1999) regression evidence that the labor movement of nationals is affected by the patterns of migration and hence the impact on the national labor market needs to be considered shows that only 4 percent of the decline in the real wage of high-school-educated workers can be attributed (and the cross-state regression evidence was apparently driven by the experience of California).

At the same time, there are powerful pressures by employers who are seeking to fill jobs. As documented in a recent work summarizing research on U.S.-Mexican immigration (Massey, Durand, and Malone 2002), the United States, for instance, has been in an awkward political equilibrium for some time: Immigration is unpopular, but there is insufficient political will to actually enforce the law, so that once workers are here, they can find work (but without an array of legal protections). Without the political will to punish employers, illegal immigration continues.[17]

So the basic idea would be to have a system (as is already operational in some domains in the United States and other countries) for labor mobility that relied on having quotas for occupational classifications, possibly specific to labor market "areas."[18] This would involve the following:

—There would need to be some procedure whereby potential employers could certify a labor market "shortage" (say, by producing evidence of being unable to fill vacancies) of X thousand jobs—a procedure that can be openly contested, say by labor unions or other interested parties as part of an administrative decision.

—These labor market shortages could be aggregated up and then allocated across countries—so that country Z would then have permission to send some fraction of the X thousand workers for Y years with permission to work in those specific labor market positions (though with some flexibility across firms).

—The labor market allocations would be up for review after a fixed period, at which time the allocation could be expanded or contracted.

In large part, this system would address both general distributional concerns about the "loss of jobs" and specific concerns about "enclaves" of unassimilated workers. That is, if there is some process whereby it is acknowledged that these workers are "needed" for a certain local industry, then it is more likely that one can build local support for tolerance (if not acceptance). To some extent, this already happens in the United States in industries like agriculture, where it is widely acknowledged that reliance on (currently illegal) workers is essential to the survival of the local sector, and hence even large

---

17. This is exacerbated by the periodic, time-inconsistent "amnesties" that give access to citizenship to individuals who flaunted the law and stayed in the country illegally—not to mention the fraudulent claims of continuous residence or past occupation (Massey, Durand, and Malone 2002).

18. The United States had a program like this, the *bracero* program, which operated for twenty-two years (from 1942 to 1964), involving almost 5 million Mexican immigrants who worked almost exclusively in agriculture (Massey, Durand, and Malone 2002).

flows of unassimilated workers are tolerated. One suspects that a lack of assimilation and distribution across sectors in the labor market is a potentially more volatile combination—though this is an area of considerable uncertainty.

There are two possible modes for a scheme of this type: a domestic employer mode, and a foreign contractor mode. The employer mode involves putting the onus on employers in a given industry to establish their business need and inability to find local workers (similar to the process for H-1B visas in the United States, for example). One would then open a fixed number work permits that are occupation specific for workers (allocated across source countries) and leave the process of matching the individuals with jobs up to the individual and employers. In the United States, in many industries that employ foreign workers, this is in some way the de facto system if one construes "permission" to enter the country as control of the border and employers are freed from any real threat of enforcement (Borjas 1999).

An alternative is to allow "labor mobility brokers" to have licenses to supply a given number of workers for specific occupations. In this way, the recruiting, matching with jobs, and transporting are the responsibility of a foreign firm, not individuals, and the matching is done in the *sending* country. In this case, the legal *employment* relationship is with a domestic firm, but all hiring has to be carried out via one of many licensed labor brokers. In many cases, this is how it is done currently in practice, but the fact that it is mostly illegal means that workers are even at more risk of being exploited and abused (see below).

A third approach is to follow the model of "services trade" and have sending-country firms enter into agreements to provide certain services, with the right to bring in their own employees to do the work. In this case, the recruiting and matching with jobs are done in the sending country, the employment relationship is between a sending-country firm and the workers, and the host-country firm enters into a contracting relationship with only the sending-country firm (and has no "employment" relationship with workers).

Some variant of these three approaches could be used for different situations, depending on the occupation (for example, construction work versus domestic help versus cleaning services versus restaurant workers). I mildly favor the intermediate approach of having "labor mobility brokers" for two main reasons. First, by making the return of individuals the broker's responsibility, at least part of the difficulty of return is shared by the foreign-based labor broker. Having a limited number of licensed brokers that the domestic-country agencies deal with on enforcement is an advantage over making domestic agencies responsible for each individual foreign worker's return. Moreover, strictly domestic-country employer responsibility for return is politically difficult. The "grand bargains" struck for better access for employers to foreign workers in exchange for participation in enforcement, as was envisioned in the 1986 reforms in the United States, never seem to last, because ex post it is politically difficult to punish domestic employers.

Second, the procedure of using labor brokers makes it easier to protect worker rights in the receiving countries rather than having just individual relationships between workers and domestic employers because it creates multiple checks and balances. The "foreign labor contractor" approach exempts the host-country employer and government almost totally from responsibility for abuses.

Accommodation Four: Enhancing the Development Impact of Migration

Migration has traditionally been seen as a neutral or negative force in development (or merely as a sign that development has failed). The very phrase "brain drain" referring to the emigration of skilled persons implies a negative. The permanent movement of unskilled labor is regarded as roughly neutral. The only item that has sometimes been considered a positive is remittances, but even though remittances are estimated to be of the same order as all foreign aid flows, the literature on the potential growth impact is small.

Because many recent publications on migration have emphasized remittances, it is important to get this straight. In chapter 1, table 1-4 on the estimates of the general equilibrium gains from labor mobility stressed that nearly all the benefits accrue to the movers, which is in part what makes the political economy difficult. The World Bank's *Global Economic Prospects 2006* (World Bank 2005a) also presents estimates of the gains from migration from a general equilibrium model, reproduced as table 4-3. In these estimates, the gains to those in sending countries in private consumption are, strikingly, larger than those to the migrants themselves (131 billion versus 126 billion). The report clarifies: "A significant portion of the gain is due to remittances from new migrants, with some improvement in labor market conditions for remaining workers" (p. 34). While emphasizing the gains to "natives in developing countries" clearly plays up the "development" impact of migration, to my mind there is only a very slight conceptual distinction. Take a hypothetical couple, of which only one spouse works. Suppose they move together to a new country. There are no "remittances," and all the benefit is attributed to the "new migrant." Now, suppose the spouse is not allowed to move, the working spouse moves and makes exactly the same amount more, and the spending of each person in the couple is exactly the same (and suppose they split their income 50–50). Is now somehow the gain divided between "new migrants" and "natives of developing countries"? Does the fact that the sharing of household income requires cross-border movement of money (remittances) make it

Table 4-3. *Distribution of Income Gains from Labor Force Expansion across Country Income Groups*[a]
Billions of U.S. dollars

Group	Private	Public	Total
Natives in high-income countries	139	−1	138
Old migrants in high-income countries	−88	0	−88
Natives in developing countries	131	12	143
New migrants	126	36	162
World total	308	47	355

Source: Adapted from table 2.3 in World Bank 2005a.
a. Real income gains (adjusted for cost of living) from an expansion in labor movement of 3 percent of high-income country labor force.

better somehow? In my view, if couples were allowed to live together and hence remittances fell dramatically, this would be an improvement. This is why I am reluctant to place too much stress on "remittances" as a reason for allowing labor mobility. At the same time, it is true that the perception is that "remittances" are "good for development" while people moving is not—even though the impact on *nationals'* income is exactly the same—because of the nation-state bias in development discourse.

I suspect that part of the reason migration has not been regarded as a *development* issue is that many of its benefits mostly elude the control of the sending-country government.[19] Once workers have earnings abroad, it is difficult to bring them back into official channels. Taxing workers on their earnings abroad is nigh impossible. Hence, one reason that migration might not have been strongly on the international agenda is that the developing-country governments themselves perceive little benefit in migration. Of course, there are good reasons to be nervous about getting sending-country governments involved in migration. Many migrants are leaving precisely because of poor governance in their home countries. Getting those very governments whose citizens are anxious to depart involved in internationally negotiated agreements to control migration, collect taxes, and hold forced savings is not an obvious winner of an idea.[20]

19. However, leaders in Latin America, such as Mexican president Vicente Fox, are increasingly taking up migration policy as an important political issue.
20. A scheme of this type in Mexico, a reasonably well-governed country, ended up in protracted legal disputes.

However, not having labor mobility perceived as an antidevelopment issue reduces its political support in host countries. As pointed out above, in none of the popular movements or policy advocacy has migration been a positive issue. Watching the coverage of the "Live Eight" concerts in July 2005, for instance, I was struck by how much enthusiasm could be generated for placing more resources under the control of African governments (more aid, debt relief), while apparently none at all could be generated for allowing Africans themselves to come in person and work. In fact, a fair bit of development advocacy is taken up in *fighting* brain drain–type recruitment, as in the recruitment of medical personnel from Africa.

How could migration policies be made more development friendly? The first step would be to make the allocation of country quotas for employment more "development friendly" by choosing a broader range of countries, depending on their needs. That is, if "migration" is thought of as at least in part development assistance along the lines of trade preferences, then part of the quotas could be allocated to the poorest countries. This is probably the main avenue by which these schemes could become more development friendly— just by increasing the incomes of at least some individuals from very poor countries.

For a *given* type of employment from a given country, what can be done to increase development friendliness? Sending-country governments could first be given some (small) share in the tax take of their citizens' earnings while abroad. If temporary migration were broad in the ambit of legality, then collecting social security or pension taxes would be feasible. Because temporary workers may earn only limited pension benefits, remitting those to the individual or to the sending-country government is perhaps feasible (though of course this depends on local tax laws). The retention of those revenues until the mover returns is also another mechanism of inducing compliance with the temporary stay (though again, alone as an incentive it will likely not be effective).

Second, a key issue is how to enhance the development impact of remittances (de la Garza and Lowell 2002). Measures to make the market for remittances work more effectively to drive costs down are one obvious direction (World Bank 2005a). More broadly, often the interest of migrants in working abroad is precisely to accumulate savings for specific purchases. A greater portion of remittance flows support consumption directly. Moreover, even what savings accrue are allegedly not always invested in productive ways—but this is often because the investment climate is unattractive or governments are predatory, so "hiding" the savings in housing is attractive. Though the prospect of forcing migrants to pay remittances into some government scheme for investment is not at all promising, if the development impact of migration is to be enhanced, one of the key channels will be to create savings schemes whereby a certain fraction of a worker's earnings are held in escrow and returned to the worker only upon return to the home country (partly as an enforcement)—but then the question is how to channel those escrow funds into productive investments.

Another promising avenue is to facilitate the participation of migrants in making entirely voluntary contributions to development projects in their home villages and communities. For instance, a social fund program in El Salvador has a provision for expatriate contributions of matching funds to local public goods (for example, schools, water projects). Again, it is important that these be voluntary rather than compulsory to prevent abuse and waste.

A third question of development impact is whether work abroad translates into future trade and business linkages. Though the focus is on "unskilled" labor from the point of view of the receiving country, in many countries individuals with high school degrees or higher are actually highly skilled relative to their market but "unskilled" in the developed-country market.[21]

A fourth question is how a temporary spell of working abroad changes a person's opinions, views—broadly put, is there a positive "empowerment" impact of work abroad, or not? If not, could something feasibly be done at low cost to create such an impact?

Although the details are to be worked out, the basic idea is to strengthen wherever possible the link between the higher wages paid to *nationals* because they are allowed to work in rich countries as part of a temporary migration scheme and the well-being of the *nation-state* from whence they came.

Accommodation Five: Sending-Country Participation in Enforcement

Sending-country enforcement is necessary if "temporary" is really to be temporary. If the sending-country government has no interest in migrants coming back, it is very difficult for the host-country government to overcome the desire between migrants and employers to collude (as is the case with enforcing laws against any "victimless" crime; if migrants want to work and employers want to hire, then both parties are satisfied, except for abuses, with illegality). But to get sending-country enforcement requires sending-country benefits. How sending-country enforcement works depends on the scheme—but schemes with labor brokers or contractors are an avenue for sending-

---

21. No one working on migration who lives on the East Coast can fail to have hundreds of personal examples. On a flight home from Washington, the person inspecting my bags as a contract hire of the security service was an Ethiopian man who had been an aircraft mechanic for Ethiopian Air.

country government to be involved. Of course, the real risk is that many sending-country governments are abusive and corrupt and would take advantage of any participation in a labor export scheme to extract benefits from the workers. In many countries, labor brokers and governments collude to exploit workers, so a large part of the gains from moving abroad are skimmed from the worker to the broker and governments that control and ration access to the schemes.

Bilateral schemes should have sending-country engagement in enforcement of the quotas (which is made easy with one-for-one reductions in the flow allowed in any year for any nonreturnees) but also receiving-country enforcement of the process of choosing eligible migrants and of broker fees. There will be more on this below.

Accommodation Six: Why "Protect Fundamental Human Rights"?

It is hard to think of groups more vulnerable than international migrants— they often move illegally and so have no recourse to legal systems to protest abuses; they end up in countries where they do not speak the language or know the culture and are often at the not-so-tender mercy of "dealers" or "contractors" (called pejoratively "traffickers" when the exchanges are illegal) or employers. History is replete with examples of horrific abuses of migrant labor. Some of the opposition to migration is the idea that migration is not really "voluntary" but rather a "tragic choice"—not a positive decision by people seeking opportunity but rather something people are forced into by the lack of any alternative (which leads to a focus on *reducing* migration as an objective). Certainly, under the current system of illegal and hence informal migration, many people are forced into tragic choices—which is why proposals for expanding labor mobility must emphasize that, within the legal schemes, moving across borders is an opportunity and not a tragic necessity.

It might be perceived as heartless to refer to protecting fundamental human rights as an "accommodation," because I regard it as absolutely central in its own right to protect human beings from abuse. But I am emphasizing this as "accommodation" because of the curious political coalition needed to sustain support for labor mobility, a coalition perhaps best illustrated with an anecdote. When I was working on this monograph, I attended a conference in Europe of mixed American and European academics (most not economists). In discussing labor mobility, I tried to emphasize that the position that conveyed concern for the *world's* poor was greater labor mobility—and in any case, there was a looming labor shortage in Europe. The Europeans by and large thought that concern for *Europe's* poor meant that the proper "left" or socially progressive stance should be against labor mobility because a "labor shortage" merely meant that real wages for the lesser skilled were increasing. As these positions were staked out, an economist living in Los Angeles piped up and said, "What do you mean there is no labor shortage, have you tried to hire a good gardener in Los Angeles?" This intervention, perhaps meant as support for my position, undermined it completely because it convinced the Europeans that labor mobility was indeed a plot by employers and the rich to exploit domestic labor by threatening them with imported workers.

The political coalition that will support temporary labor mobility will include employers, but to succeed it also has to include socially progressive forces that support labor mobility because of its beneficial effects for the world's poor. At the risk of caricature, I would conjecture that protecting human rights will not be at the top of the agenda of potential employers that support expanded labor mobility. But while the socially progressive forces will be convinced of the necessity to protect human rights within any scheme of labor movement because it is the right thing to do, even the most heartless employers can be convinced to support the protection of human rights to promote the schemes politically.

Currently, many of the worst abuses of migrants arise precisely because of the illegal nature of the activity or, because legal channels are precluded, there is illegal human trafficking, such as across borders for prostitution. One goal of any systemic reform of migration is to move all cross-border flows into legal channels and thus allow a complete crackdown on illegal moves across borders. If only a fraction of the enforcement expenditures currently undertaken—for instance, to prevent Mexicans from getting ordinary jobs as domestic workers or gardeners—were devoted to preventing human trafficking for illegal purposes, the gains would likely be large.

But this "grand bargain" that includes the protection of human rights requires that employers in the host countries cooperate. This is why having a procedure to declare labor scarcity is crucial. Only if employers feel they have a legal mechanism for meeting what they feel are their legitimate demands for labor will a consensus emerge and enforcement be possible. The move to legality and protecting against abuses also might be another reason to move to sending-country labor brokers (again, in spite of the risks), as there is more possibility that they themselves will work to eliminate competition from illegal senders. Also, labor brokers make enforcement easier because they can be suspended from business, and because they would have to register in both sending and receiving countries, they can be controlled on both ends.

Even with encouragement to cooperate by host-country employers and sending-country labor brokers (if they are used), there needs to be a built-in mechanism for reporting abuses by employers and by brokers. This mechanism needs to have the participation of both sending and host countries (host countries cannot rely exclusively on sending countries to patrol their own brokers). Penalties for abuse must be built into the system for employers, brokers, and sending countries (for example, losing rights to future flows).

Summary of Temporary Schemes

Table 4-4 summarizes the analysis by matching the accommodations to the specific anti-labor-mobility ideas that they are meant to overcome. This section does not make specific proposals, for these need to be tailored to the specific circumstances of each country, but rather indicate what are likely desirable features of the class of proposals for increased labor mobility that are politically acceptable. There are proposals that meet all or most of these broad principles on the agenda, either in specific instances or as a broader part of "globalization." For instance, Massey, Durand, and Malone (2002) propose the issuance of 300,000 two-year visas for *temporary* Mexican immigration. Rodrik (2002) proposes to add a scheme for temporary work visas to the international agenda based on many of the same concerns as articulated here.[22]

Outside the OECD countries, these programs are common. A recent study by Kremer and Watt (2006) examines the case of foreign domestic helpers. In Singapore and Hong Kong, these were roughly 7 percent of the total labor force (compared, for instance, with only 0.3 percent in the United States). These programs are very much a "temporary labor mobility" scheme because they are strictly controlled by the receiving countries, involve quotas on those admitted, limit the recruited women to the occupation of household worker, and usually involve bilateral relationships with sending governments. Kremer and Watt estimate the gain to the host country from this program as between 1.3 and 3.3 percent of national income. Moreover, because fiscal costs are limited (recruited women are not allowed to bring children, for instance), and because the provision of domestic help raises the labor force participation rate of skilled women, there are enormous fiscal gains (not fiscal losses). They note

---

22. Since I began working on this manuscript (alas, several years ago), some new proposals have emerged in the United States, including one from the George W. Bush administration. I am not going to address the specifics of these proposals, for several reasons. First, this book is primarily about the stance the development community should take toward labor mobility, not about policies in just one country. Second, it is impossible to discuss specific proposals without attracting partisan heat that is unproductive in the present context. Third, there are distinct issues of agreeing on general principles and the desirability of schemes of a general type. Because people in the development community are far from agreeing on the general principles, discussion of whether a specific proposal meets those principles is premature.

Table 4-4. *Schemes for Temporary Mobility of Unskilled Labor*

Proposal	Schemes for temporary mobility of unskilled labor	Summary
Five forces for increased labor mobility		
High and rising wage gaps	+	Allows workers some access to high wages
Differing demographic destinies	+	Limited impact as magnitude of problem is too large
Everything but labor globalization	+	Brings labor at least into bilateral relations
Employment growth in hard-core nontradable services	+	Singles out industries/occupations for quotas
Ghost/zombie countries	+	Employment quotas can be allocated to poorest countries
Eight ideas limiting migration in industrial countries		
Nationality is a morally legitimate basis for discrimination	+	Accommodation 1—unilateral control of agreements
Moral perfectionism based on "proximity"	+	Accommodation 6—protect human rights of workers
"Development" is exclusively about nation-states, not nationals.	+	Accommodation 4—making schemes as "development friendly" as possible
Labor movements are not "necessary" (or desirable) to raise living standards	+	
Increased migration of unskilled labor will lower wages and worsen the distribution of income in the receiving countries	+	Accommodation 3—occupation (and region) specific quotas to reduce job displacement
Movers are a fiscal cost as they use more services than they pay in taxes	+	Accommodation 2—temporary workers only
Allowing movement across borders creates risks of crime and terrorism	+	Accommodation 1—unilateral agreements can specify nationality and conditions for entry
"They" are not like "us"—culture clash	−/+	Accommodation 2—temporary means less cultural/political influence—but migrants are not "incorporated" and risks backlash

that if the United States were to initiate such a program that allowed the proportion of the labor force in this category to reach the levels of Singapore or Hong Kong and each woman remitted $5,000 each year, this would make for remittances of $40 billion annually—more than four times U.S. development assistance. Of course, these programs do often raise concerns about whether basic human rights are protected, but innovative programs in the sending countries are addressing the risks of abuse.

Working out the details for specific countries will require a substantial amount of work; readers will notice that all the details are left to be filled in: What is the process whereby the numbers for the quotas will be chosen? By which agencies? Who will regulate the contracts? Who will promote the "development" aspects? What fraction of taxes will be remitted, and to whom? Who will hold the savings in escrow? How will the rights of workers be protected? Many similar schemes have failed on these details, for that is where the devil resides.

Conclusion

In a democracy, every public policy requires some accommodations from what experts might conceive of as the "technocratic" ideal—military bases are diversified across constituencies, regulatory policy responds to public perceptions, highways are routed (or rerouted), import "safeguard" policies are adopted—to adjust to political pressures. There is no reason to expect that policy toward who is allowed to work in a country should be any different. The free market ideals of cosmopolitan globalizing economists of "let anyone come who wants to" has *no* political constituency. The enormous unpopularity of "immigration" as an issue in nearly every rich country guarantees that the accommodations will be large. The current "accommodation" that reconciles forces and ideas in many countries is denial—so migration is pushed underground and into an informal and shadow economy. This imposes large costs on the migrants and creates, in the long run, substantial political resentment and backlash, tainting all labor mobility with the broad strokes of illegitimacy.

As can be seen, the accommodations as part of a feasible increase in unskilled labor mobility make enormous sacrifices. Table 4-5 compares the three broad classes of policy proposals. The temporary schemes lose some of the economically attractive features of some policies, such as binding commitments to "market access" under the WTO, and try to eliminate some of the features of the "high-quality migrant" schemes that make them politically popular but unfriendly to development. Moreover, the accommodations tend

Table 4-5. *Summary of the Classes of Proposals for Increasing Labor Mobility*[a]

Proposal	Increased emphasis on high skill/wealth	GATS mode 4 within WTO	Schemes for temporary mobility of unskilled labor
Five forces for increased labor mobility			
High and rising wage gaps	−	+	+
Differing demographic destinies	+		+
Everything but labor globalization	−	+++	+
Employment growth in hard-core nontradable services	+/−	+++	+
Ghost/zombie countries	−		+
Eight ideas limiting migration in industrial countries			
Nationality is a morally legitimate basis for discrimination	+++	− − −	+
Moral perfectionism based on "proximity"	++		+
"Development" is exclusively about nation-states, not nationals	− −	+++	+
Labor movements are not "necessary" (or desirable) to raise living standards	− −	−	
Increased migration of unskilled labor will lower wages and worsen the distribution of income in the receiving countries	+++	− − −	+
Movers are a fiscal cost as they use more services than they pay in taxes	+++	+/−	+
Allowing movement across borders creates risks of crime and terrorism	+++	− − − −	+
"They" are not like "us"— culture clash	+	− − −	+/−
Summary	Politically feasible, not the most development friendly	Development friendly, not politically feasible	With accommodations, a bit of both

a. GATS = General Agreement on Trade in Services; WTO = World Trade Organization to violate nearly every principle economists hold dear—let markets operate; intervene with price instruments, not quotas; keep bad governments' hands off as many transactions as possible; and allow people the maximum choice—for political viability.

But while the difficulties are immense, the potential gains are enormous. For instance, the projected *incremental* growth in low-skill, hard-core non-tradable services in the United States over the next ten years is 5 million jobs (see chapter 1). From one data set, the average gain to migrants to the United States with a high school education or less was about $8,000 annually (Rosen-zweig 2004). Suppose that the composition of employment growth in other OECD countries over the next decade is similar to that of the United States, and suppose that the United States has about a third of total employment growth and that the wage gains are similar. Then, in 2010, there will be 15 million low-skill, hard-core nontradable jobs. If, through the use of schemes of the type proposed here, only 10 percent of these *incremental* jobs were held by poor-country citizens, the income gains would be 1.5 million times $8,000, or $12 billion—already a significant fraction of all development assistance. If, again due to the development of politically acceptable schemes, 50 percent of the increment (again, not half the total, just half the growth) could be taken up by poor-country citizens and 7.5 million additional people (still only a small addition to the OECD labor force) could work at these wages than would have in the absence of these schemes, then the net direct benefit to poor people would be $60 billion a year—roughly the value of all current foreign aid, and if handled correctly, with net *benefits* rather than costs to the receiving countries. Advancing policies for increased unskilled labor mobility will not be easy. But for even these modest gains, it would all be worth it.

5

Conclusion: Let Their People Come

B ecause the arguments in this monograph have been painfully simple and, I hope, clear, I need not devote too much space to a summary, which boils down to three points:

—There are five irresistible forces in the global economy creating growing pressures for greater movement of labor across national borders, particularly from poorer to richer countries.

—These forces are met by the immovable ideas of rich-country citizens who oppose such movements, with the result that although mobility has increased somewhat, labor mobility is suppressed.

—Proposals for development-friendly labor mobility policies will have to work to accommodate the immovable ideas in the interests of increased flows.

This gives space for a conclusion to address the question of why anyone—policymaker, politician, policy advocacy group, or global citizen—should become the champion of policies for development-friendly migration. After all, in many countries, the "increase migration" voters are outnumbered by five to one or even ten to one by voters who would prefer to "reduce migration." Wise and pragmatic people often deliberately ignore insurmountable problems to surmount the surmountable. Perhaps increasing flows of unskilled labor from poor countries in a systematic way, even if it would be enormously beneficial to the world's poor, is simply insurmountable. Perhaps a modest amount of charity work for those trapped in poor countries is all that can be surmounted. Clearly, any proposal for "open borders" or "free immigration" is simply pointless. But it is worth asking if there are not modest steps that can be taken toward realizing the potential benefits. The question is: When?

The "founders" of the post–World War II international political and economic structure have to be thanked, especially by anyone who lives in a country belonging to the Organization for Economic Cooperation and Development (OECD). The years from 1945 to 2005 stand out as perhaps the best sixty years for human material progress in history. The postwar founders created institutions to promote the increased mobility of goods. They created institutions to facilitate capital movements. But people were frozen. Any restrictions governments chose to place on the movement of persons—including banning entry, banning exit, banning movement within a country, or even, to a lesser extent, forced migrations and resettlements within a country—are, within some broad limits, simply outside the scope of international concern. Institutions were created to resolve conflicts among nation-states. Organizations were created to promote the economic progress of nation-states. But there has been almost no systematic pressure for improving the conditions for the movements of people to pursue economic opportunity.

A "Burkean progressive" combines a deep aversion to throwing out babies with the bathwater with an optimistic belief that the bathwater can nevertheless be cleaned.[1] The postwar systems have demonstrated that international systems that create pressures for gradual change, are allowed to adapt, and devise mechanisms for adjudicating disputes and resolving conflicts can achieve enormous results over time. The success of the General Agreement on Tariffs and Trade in weaning the OECD, and then the rest of the world, from pre–World War II protectionism and toward a liberalized trade regime through protracted rounds of negotiation has been truly startling. Yet the

---

1. One debate the history of the twentieth century should have settled once and for all is the "revolutionary" versus the "incrementalist" approaches to improving the human condition. The most grisly and tragic episodes of the twentieth century are those in which an inspired leader pursued a radical and revolutionary program that attempted to remake an entire system in a new image of human nature—Hitler, Stalin, Mao, Pol Pot, and Kim Il Sung all had a vision they believed to be for the betterment of humankind that could be achieved quickly. Even a cursory comparison of Chinese history from 1949 to 1976 versus 1978 to the present suggests the huge advantages of creative tinkering and forceful muddling through over "great" leaps of any kind.

postwar international system has no labor mobility equivalent of the International Monetary Fund, which serves as an international guarantor and advocate for the international system of payments, successfully maintaining an orderly system of international payments (even when the previous Bretton Woods arrangements broke down). Even if migration policies are to be set bilaterally, the creation of an international organization—perhaps the World Migration Organization, as proposed recently by Jagdish Bhagwati (2003)—would be a feasible step.

Although keeping labor mobility off the international agenda may have been a wise choice by the postwar founders, given their immediate conditions and thinking, the question must be asked: How long should the world wait? How long after free trade is promoted before people should also be at least freer to move? How long after capital is free to move before people are allowed? How long should transfers through aid be the only mechanism for promoting development? How long must *only* Bolivia, Armenia, or Nigeria figure on the international agenda and *not* Bolivi*ans*, Armeni*ans*, or Nigeri*ans*. *When* does one conclude that migration can, and must, come onto the development agenda, and *how* is this made a surmountable problem?

Fortunately, the "when" question has an answer. The "development community" has put itself on the clock. The Millennium Development Goals (MDGs) are specific, measurable, time-bound goals. These ambitious goals, which have been signed off on by all major agencies and donor governments, propose between 1990 and 2015 halving poverty, achieving universal completion of primary schooling, equalizing school enrollments by gender, reducing infant mortality by two-thirds, and the like. We are about exactly at the midpoint of this period, and it is obvious that the MDGs are unlikely to be achieved in every country (although it is conceivable that some or even most of them will be achieved in the world aggregate, depending on what happens in India and China).

Two recent reports on the MDGs—by the UN Millennium Project (United Nations 2005) and the Commission for Africa (2005)—are state-of-the-art efforts resulting from high-profile international exercises involving impressive analytical minds and top-ranking politicians. They both emphasize the need to accelerate progress in the poorest countries, especially in Africa, if the MDGs are to be met. Both of them emphasize the traditional means by which the "international community" can contribute to meeting the MDGs—primarily more and better aid, better market access, and more support for global public goods. In both reports, the issue of migration is next to invisible—especially any suggestion that rich countries could allow more unskilled labor to immigrate. In the 356 pages of the UN report, "migration" (or variants) is mentioned twenty-one times, of which exactly one is a suggestion about progress in the General Agreement on Trade in Services mode 4 in the Doha round multilateral trade negotiations and the rest frame "migration" as a problem—of "brain drain," as a cause of conflict, or as an urbanization issue causing pressures on urban infrastructure. Similarly, in the text of the Commission for Africa report, migration is mentioned eleven times, again in only one instance in the sense that the rich countries could (or should) do something positive.[2]

This is not a criticism of these reports. They faithfully mirror the political milieu in which they were produced—the Group of Eight's Gleneagles meeting. The reality is that the Group of Eight's political leaders, meeting to discuss actions to assist Africa, are enormously more likely to agree (at least in principle) to increase aid to African governments than they are to agree to admit more Africans. Moreover, the reality is that the Group of Eight's leaders were not under any pressure to reduce barriers to labor mobility—from the left or right of the political spectrum. The large effort to create a public relations effort to influence the meeting created no pressure on migration issues.

Perhaps the existing plans will succeed in reaching the MDGs and "make poverty history." Personally, I hope they do. But what if they do not? The clock is ticking on the MDGs; what is plan B? The usual plan B for ambitious development targets is some variant on squirming out—blame the "lack of commitment" as the reason for failure, or keep the same targets but lengthen the horizon (as has been done with universal primary education many times; see Clemens 2004), or gradually let the movement lose steam in favor of some new agenda.

An alternative plan B is to use the deadline for the MDGs as a focal point to bring labor mobility explicitly onto the development agenda. If, in 2010, it is clear that the MDGs will not be achieved, then an international forum (such as the Group of Eight or the World Economic Forum) and international organizations (such as the World Bank, International Monetary Fund, and United Nations) should have a plan B to begin to promote development-friendly labor mobility. Plan B is shifting from the "globalization of everything but labor" with modest financial flows to adding improved labor mobility and migration policies in rich countries explicitly to the list of instruments to promote poverty reduction.

This might be one way to create pressure on "when?" But the question is still "how?" We need to begin now, today, to develop the details of mechanisms

---

2. The paragraph outlines why rich countries will not liberalize General Agreement on Trade in Services mode 4 and concludes with a less-than-ringing call to action: "However, some modest progress could generate benefits for Sub-Saharan Africa."

of development-friendly labor mobility that are politically feasible. Perhaps these will be along the lines I have suggested here. Perhaps (actually, almost certainly) I am wrong about the specifics of the accommodations that will be needed to match the economics—which is simple—to the political economy—which is not. There is no question that steps forward will be both incremental and difficult, and they will require a political confrontation with an issue nearly everyone would just as soon avoid: What are the conditions on which it is acceptable to offer nationals of other countries the opportunity to be physically present to perform economic services?

This question is difficult to confront both because the enormous gaps in well-being across countries mean that people will be willing to migrate on terms that make rich-country citizens uncomfortable and also because it requires addressing the often-ignored differential effects of economic policy. But it is to be hoped that—just as pressure is brought to bear on leaders for greater liberalization of trade and greater financial assistance to poor nation-states—pressure can be brought to bear to finally address the missing link in the current global system, both surmounting the immovable ideas opposing and productively accommodating the irresistible forces for greater labor mobility. Eventually, the citizens of the rich world must decide on what terms they will let the world's poor people come.

References

Acemoglu, Daron. 2001. "Factor Prices and Technical Change: From Induced Innovations to Recent Debates." In *Knowledge, Information, and Expectations in Modern Macroeconomics: In Honor of Edmund Phelps,* edited by Philippe Aghion, Roman Frydman, Joseph Stiglitz, and Michael Woodford. Princeton University Press.

Acemoglu, Daron, Simon Johnson, James Robinson, and Yunyong Thaicharoen. 2003. "Institutional Causes, Macroeconomic Symptoms: Volatility, Crises And Growth." *Journal of Monetary Economics* 50: 49–123.

Anderson, Benedict. 1991. *Imagined Communities.* New York: Verso.

Baumol, William J. 1967. "Macroeconomics of Unbalanced Growth: The Anatomy of Urban Crisis." *American Economic Review* 42, no. 3: 415–26.

Bhagwati, Jagdish. 2003. "Borders beyond Control." *Foreign Affairs,* 82, no. 1: 98–104.

Birdsall, Nancy, and Lant Pritchett. 2002. "North and South in the Western Hemisphere: The Impact of Population Dynamics and Migration on Education, Wages, Inequality, and Savings." Center for Global Development, Washington.

Borjas, George. 1999. *Heaven's Door: Immigration Policy and the American Economy.* Princeton University Press.

Bourguignon, F., and C. Morrison. 2002. "Inequality among World Citizens: 1820–1992." *American Economic Review* 92, no. 4: 727–44.

Butcher, Kristin, and Anne Piehl. 1998. "Cross-City Evidence on the Relationship between Immigration and Crime." *Journal of Policy Analysis and Management* 17, no. 2: 457–93.

Card, David. 1990. "The Impact of the Mariel Boatlift on the Miami Labor Market." *Industrial and Labor Relations Review* 43, no. 3: 245–57.

Carens, Joseph. 1987. "Aliens and Citizens: The Case for Open Borders." *Review of Politics* 49: 251–73.

Clemens, Michael. 2004. *The Long Walk to School: International Education Goals in Historical Perspective.* Center for Global Development Working Paper 37. Washington.

Cline, William. 2005. *Trade Policy and Global Poverty*. Washington: Institute for International Economics and Center for Global Development.

Cohen, Daniel. 2005. *Globalization and Its Enemies*. MIT Press.

Collier, Paul, Anne Hoeffler, and Catherine Pattillo. 2004. "Africa's Exodus: Capital Flight and Brain Drain as Portfolio Decisions." *Journal of African Economies* 13 (supplement): 15–54.

Commander, Simon, Mari Kangasniemi, and L. Alan Winters. 2003. "The Brain Drain: Curse or Boon?" Discussion Paper 809. Bonn: IZA.

Commission for Africa. 2005. *Our Common Interest*. London.

Davis, Stephen. 1992. "Cross Country Patterns of Change in Relative Wages." In *NBER Macroeconomics Annual 1992*. MIT Press.

De la Garza, Rodolfo, and Briant Lowell. 2002. *Sending Money Home: Hispanic Remittances and Community Development*. Lanham, Md.: Roman & Littlefield.

Demeny, Paul. 2003. "Population Policy Dilemmas in Europe at the Dawn of the Twenty-First Century." *Population and Development Review* 29, no. 1: 1–28.

Easterly, William. 2004. "Channels from Globalization to Inequality: Productivity World vs. Factor World." In *Brookings Trade Forum 2004*, edited by S. Collins. Brookings.

Easterly, William, and Ross Levine. 2002. "It's Not Factor Accumulation: Stylized Facts and Growth Models." *World Bank Economic Review* 15: 177–219.

———. 2003. "Tropics, Germs, and Crops: How Endowments Influence Economic Development." *Journal of Monetary Economics* 50, no. 1: 3–39.

Faini, Riccardo. 2001. "Development, Trade, and Migration." International Monetary Fund, Washington.

Ferguson, James. 1994. *The Anti-Politics Machine*. University of Minnesota Press.

Friedman, Thomas. 2005. *The World Is Flat: A Brief History of the 21st Century*. New York: Farrar, Straus & Giroux.

Gardner, Howard. 1991. *The Unschooled Mind: How Children Think and How Schools Should Teach*. New York: Basic Books.

Gellner, E. 1983. *Nations and Nationalism*. Cornell University Press.

Goldin, Ian, and Andrew Beath. Forthcoming. "International Migration." In *Princeton Encyclopedia of the World Economy*, edited by R. S. Rajan and K. A. Reinert. Princeton University Press.

Hamilton, Robert, and John Whalley. 1984. "Efficiency and Distributional Implications of Global Restrictions on Labor Mobility." *Journal of Developmental Economics* 14: 61–75.

Hatton, Timothy, and Jeffrey Williamson. 1998. *The Age of Mass Migration: Causes and Economic Impact*. Oxford University Press.

———. 2006. *Global Migration and the World Economy: Two Centuries of Policy and Performance*. MIT Press.

International Organization for Migration. 2005. *World Migration 2005: Costs and Benefits of International Migration*. Geneva.

Jasso, Guillermina, Mark R. Rosenzweig, and James P. Smith. 2003. "The Earnings of U.S. Immigrants: World Skill Prices, Skill Transferability, and Selectivity." Available at http://econwpa.wustl.edu:80/eps/lab/papers/0312/0312007.pdf.

Kapur, Davesh, and John McHale. 2005. *Give Us Your Best and Brightest*. Washington: Center for Global Development.

Katz, Lawrence F., and K. M. Murphy. 1992. "Changes in Relative Wages, 1963–87: Supply and Demand Factors." *Quarterly Journal of Economics* 107, no. 1: 35–78.

King, Robert G., and Sergio T. Rebelo. 1993. "Transitional Dynamics and Economic Growth in the Neoclassical Model." *American Economic Review* 83, no. 4: 908–31, September.

Klenow, Peter, and Andres Rodriguez-Clare. 1997. "The Neoclassical Revival: Has It Gone Too Far?" In *NBER Macroeconomics Annual 1997* (National Bureau of Economic Research), edited by Ben S. Bernanke and Julio Rotemberg. MIT Press.

Kremer, Michael, and Stanley Watt. 2006. "The Globalization of Household Production." Harvard University.

Lawrence, Robert. 2004. *Has Globalization Gone Far Enough?* Washington: Institute for International Economics.

Lindert, Peter. 2005. *Growing Public: Social Spending and Economic Growth since the Eighteenth Century.* Cambridge University Press.

Maddison, Angus. 1995. *Monitoring the World Economy, 1820–1992.* Paris: Organization for Economic Cooperation and Development.

———. 2001. *The World Economy: A Millennial Perspective.* Paris: Organization for Economic Cooperation and Development.

Martin, Philip. 2004. "*Migration.*" In *Global Crisis, Global Solutions,* edited by Bjorn Lomborg. Cambridge University Press.

Massey, Douglas S., Joaquin Arango, Graeme Hugo, Ali Kouaouci, Adela Pellegrino, and J. Edward Taylor. 1999. *Worlds in Motion: Understanding International Migration at the End of the Millennium.* Oxford University Press.

Massey, Douglas S., Jorge Durand, and Nolan J. Malone. 2002. *Beyond Smoke and Mirrors: Mexican Immigration in an Era of Economic Integration.* New York: Russell Sage Foundation.

Mayda, Anna Maria. 2002. "Who Is Against Immigration?" Harvard University.

McKenzie, David, John Gibson, and Steven Stillman. 2006. *How Important Is Selection? Experimental vs. Non-Experimental Measures of the Income Gains from Migration.* Bonn: IZA.

Milanovic, Branko. 2003. "Globalization and Goals: Does Soccer Show the Way?" Carnegie Endowment for International Peace, Washington.

National Research Council. 1997. "The New Americans: Economic, Demographic, and Fiscal Effects of Immigration." In *Panel on the Demographic and Economic Impacts of Immigration,* edited by James P. Smith and Barry Edmonston. Washington: National Academies Press.

Nozick, Robert. 1974. *Anarchy, State, and Utopia.* New York: Basic Books.

Nussbaum, Martha. 2006. *Frontiers of Justice: Disability, Nationality, Species Membership.* Harvard University Press.

OECD. 2004. *Trends in International Migration and Migration Policies.* Paris: Organization for Economic Cooperation and Development.

O'Rourke, Kevin H., and Richard Sinnott. 2003. "Migration Flows: Political Economy of Migration and the Empirical Challenges." Institute for International Integration Studies Discussion Paper 6. Dublin: Trinity College.

O'Rourke, Kevin, and Jeffrey Williamson. 1999. *Globalization and History: The Evolution of a Nineteenth-Century Atlantic Economy.* MIT Press.

Pritchett, Lant. 1997. "Divergence, Big Time." *Journal of Economic Perspectives* 11: 3–17.

———. 2001. "Where Has All the Education Gone?" *World Bank Economic Review* 15, no. 3: 367–91.

———. 2004a. "Boom Towns and Ghost Countries: Geography, Agglomeration, and Population Mobility." Working Paper 36. Washington: Center for Global Development.

———. 2004b. "Does Learning to Add Up Add Up? The Returns to Schooling in Aggregate Data." BREAD Working Paper 53. Bureau for Research in Economic Analysis of Development, Center for International Development, Harvard University.

———. 2006. "Who Is Not Poor? Dreaming of a World Truly Free of Poverty." *World Bank Research Observer* 26, no. 1: 1–23.

Rama, Martin, and Raquel Artecona. 2002. "A Database of Labor Market Indicators." World Bank, Washington.

Rawls, John. 1970. *A Theory of Justice.* Harvard University Press.

Rodrik, Dani. 1997. *Has Globalization Gone Too Far?* Washington: Institute for International Economics.

———. 2002. "Feasible Globalizations." Harvard University.

Rodrik, Dani, Arvind Subramanian, and Francesco Trebbi. 2002. "Institutions Rule: The Primacy of Institutions over Geography and Integration in Economic Development." Working Paper 3643. London: Centre for Economic Policy Research.

Rosenzweig, Mark. 2004. "Comment on Migration." In *Global Crises, Global Solutions,* edited by Bjorn Lomborg. Cambridge University Press.

Sala-i-Martin, Xavier. 2002. "The Disturbing 'Rise' of World Income Inequality." Working Paper 8904. Cambridge, Mass.: National Bureau of Economic Research.

Scheve, Kenneth, and Matthew Slaughter. 2001. "Globalization and the Perceptions of American Workers." Institute for International Economics, Washington.

Timmer, Ashley, and Jeffrey G. Williamson. 1998. "Immigration Policy Prior to the Thirties: Labor Markets, Policy Interactions, and Globalization Backlash." *Population and Development Review* 24, no. 4: 739–71.

United Nations. 2005. *Investing in Development: A Practical Plan to Achieve the Millennium Development Goals.* New York.

United Nations Department of Economic and Social Affairs. 2002. *International Migration Report 2002.* New York.

Wilson, William Julius. 1996. *When Work Disappears: The World of the New Urban Poor.* New York: Vintage Books.

Winters, Alan, Terrie Walmsley, Zhen Kun Wang, and Roman Grynberg. 2002. "Negotiating the Liberalization of the Temporary Movement of Natural Persons." University of Sussex Discussion Paper 87. Brighton, U.K.

———. 2003. *Liberalizing Labor Mobility under the GATS.* Economic Paper 3. London: Commonwealth Secretariat.

World Bank. 2005a. *Global Economic Prospects: Economic Implications of Remittances and Migration.* Washington.

———. 2005b. *World Development Report 2006: Equity and Development.* New York: Oxford University Press.

———. 2006. *World Development Report 2007: Youth and Development.* New York: Oxford University Press.

Index